Introduction

Study Skills – what you need to know to pass exams!

Pause for thought

Many students might skip quickly through a page like this. After all, we all know how to revise. Do you really though?

Think about this:

"IF YOU ALWAYS DO WHAT YOU ALWAYS DO, YOU WILL ALWAYS GET WHAT YOU HAVE ALWAYS GOT."

Do you like the grades you get? Do you want to do better? If you get full marks in your assessment, then that's great! Change nothing! This section is just to help you get that little bit better than you already are.

There are two main parts to the advice on offer here. The first part highlights fairly obvious things but which are also very important. The second part makes suggestions about revision that you might not have thought about but which WILL help you.

Part 1

DOH! It's so obvious but …

Start revising in good time

Don't leave it until the last minute – this will make you panic.

Make a revision timetable that sets out work time AND play time.

Sleep and eat!

Obvious really, and very helpful. Avoid arguments or stressful things too – even games that wind you up. You need to be fit, awake and focused!

Know your place!

Make sure you know exactly **WHEN and WHERE** your exams are.

Know your enemy!

Make sure you know what to expect in the exam.

How is the paper structured?

How much time is there for each question?

What types of question are involved?

Which topics seem to come up time and time again?

Which topics are your strongest and which are your weakest?

Are all topics compulsory or are there choices?

Learn by DOING!

There is no substitute for past papers and practice papers – they are simply essential! Tackling this collection of papers and answers is exactly the right thing to be doing as your exams approach.

Part 2

People learn in different ways. Some like low light, some bright. Some like early morning, some like evening / night. Some prefer warm, some prefer cold. But everyone uses their BRAIN and the brain works when it is active. Passive learning – sitting gazing at notes – is the most INEFFICIENT way to learn anything. Below you will find tips and ideas for making your revision more effective and maybe even more enjoyable. What follows gets your brain active, and active learning works!

Activity 1 – Stop and review

Step 1

When you have done no more than 5 minutes of revision reading STOP!

Step 2

Write a heading in your own words which sums up the topic you have been revising.

Step 3

Write a summary of what you have revised in no more than two sentences. Don't fool yourself by saying, 'I know it but I cannot put it into words'. That just means you don't know it well enough. If you cannot write your summary, revise that section again, knowing that you must write a summary at the end of it. Many of you will have notebooks full of blue/black ink writing. Many of the pages will not be especially attractive or memorable so try to liven them up a bit with colour as you are reviewing and rewriting. **This is a great memory aid, and memory is the most important thing.**

Activity 2 — Use technology!

Why should everything be written down? Have you thought about 'mental' maps, diagrams, cartoons and colour to help you learn? And rather than write down notes, why not record your revision material?

What about having a text message revision session with friends? Keep in touch with them to find out how and what they are revising and share ideas and questions.

Why not make a video diary where you tell the camera what you are doing, what you think you have learned and what you still have to do? No one has to see or hear it but the process of having to organise your thoughts in a formal way to explain something is a very important learning practice.

Be sure to make use of electronic files. You could begin to summarise your class notes. Your typing might be slow but it will get faster and the typed notes will be easier to read than the scribbles in your class notes. Try to add different fonts and colours to make your work stand out. You can easily Google relevant pictures, cartoons and diagrams which you can copy and paste to make your work more attractive and **MEMORABLE**.

Activity 3 – This is it. Do this and you will know lots!

Step 1

In this task you must be very honest with yourself! Find the SQA syllabus for your subject (www.sqa.org.uk). Look at how it is broken down into main topics called MANDATORY knowledge. That means stuff you MUST know.

Step 2

BEFORE you do ANY revision on this topic, write a list of everything that you already know about the subject. It might be quite a long list but you only need to write it once. It shows you all the information that is already in your long-term memory so you know what parts you do not need to revise!

Step 3

Pick a chapter or section from your book or revision notes. Choose a fairly large section or a whole chapter to get the most out of this activity.

With a buddy, use Skype, Facetime, Twitter or any other communication you have, to play the game "If this is the answer, what is the question?". For example, if you are revising Geography and the answer you provide is "meander", your buddy would have to make up a question like "What is the word that describes a feature of a river where it flows slowly and bends often from side to side?".

Make up 10 "answers" based on the content of the chapter or section you are using. Give this to your buddy to solve while you solve theirs.

Step 4

Construct a wordsearch of at least 10 X 10 squares. You can make it as big as you like but keep it realistic. Work together with a group of friends. Many apps allow you to make wordsearch puzzles online. The words and phrases can go in any direction and phrases can be split. Your puzzle must only contain facts linked to the topic you are revising. Your task is to find 10 bits of information to hide in your puzzle but you must not repeat information that you used in Step 3. DO NOT show where the words are. Fill up empty squares with random letters. Remember to keep a note of where your answers are hidden but do not show your friends. When you have a complete puzzle, exchange it with a friend to solve each other's puzzle.

Step 5

Now make up 10 questions (not "answers" this time) based on the same chapter used in the previous two tasks. Again, you must find NEW information that you have not yet used. Now it's getting hard to find that new information! Again, give your questions to a friend to answer.

Step 6

As you have been doing the puzzles, your brain has been actively searching for new information. Now write a NEW LIST that contains only the new information you have discovered when doing the puzzles. Your new list is the one to look at repeatedly for short bursts over the next few days. Try to remember more and more of it without looking at it. After a few days, you should be able to add words from your second list to your first list as you increase the information in your long-term memory.

FINALLY! Be inspired...

Make a list of different revision ideas and beside each one write **THINGS I HAVE** tried, **THINGS I WILL** try and **THINGS I MIGHT** try. Don't be scared of trying something new.

And remember – "FAIL TO PREPARE AND PREPARE TO FAIL!"

Higher German

The course

The Higher qualification in German develops students' skills in Reading, Listening, Speaking and Writing. There are internal assessments (NABs) and a final external examination.

The course consists of three themes – lifestyles, education and work, and the wider world. Within these are more specific topics:

- *Lifestyles = Family, Friends and Society; Leisure and Healthy Living*
- *Education and work = School/College; Careers*
- *The wider world = Holidays and Travel; Tourism.*

How the course is graded

A pass in Higher German depends on two things:

- passes in the unit assessments
- the two papers you sit in May, together with the mark from your Speaking NAB.

The exam

Paper 1 (Reading and Directed Writing) lasts 1 hour 40 minutes and is worth 45 marks. You have to read a German text of 550–650 words and answer 20 marks worth of questions about it. You also have to translate into English a short section from the passage. The second task is Directed Writing, where you write 150–180 words in German based on a scenario.

- You must address 6 set bullet points in your writing.

Paper 2 (Listening & Writing) lasts 1 hour. You have to listen to an interview and answer 20 marks worth of questions about it. The writing task, worth 10 marks, is linked to the listening topic and in this you write 120 to 150 words expressing personal opinions and ideas.

Paper 3 is your Speaking NAB, a two-part (recorded) test worth 25 marks. In the first part, you select an area from the topics you have studied and give a 1½–2 minute presentation in German. Over the next 4–6 minutes you are asked questions about your presentation followed by further questions about other aspects of the themes and topics.

Reading

The emphasis here is on reading and re-reading the text. The scene is set for you in English; do not ignore this information. The German title of the passage is usually translated in the English introduction; this helps to ease you into the text.

You should read the entire text without using a dictionary. You do not need to understand every word – concentrate on getting the gist of what the text is saying.

When you have done this, go back to the beginning and read the first question. You will be told to look at a certain section of the text. Read that section again. Still refrain from using your dictionary! When you have finished reading the section, look at the questions asked. Identify and highlight the key word(s) in the question. Within the question, some of the most difficult words are translated for you – this also directs you to where to find the answer. Look at the number of marks available, as that tells you how much information you must give. Include every detail – the what, the when and the where. You do not need to answer in sentences; bullet points are acceptable.

A word in **bold** type is a sign that you must be really precise.

One word answers, a single number or time are unlikely to feature in a Higher Reading paper! For a question that asks "When **exactly** …?", you need a start **and** a finish time.

Read each question carefully; assume that many questions translate a phrase or sentence in that part of the text. When you have found it, you have found the answer to the question. Do not forget to include all the details.

Read over each answer. Does it make sense? Is all the detail there? Have you used your common sense? Just because you are sitting an exam, do not forget everything you know about life!

You will read some parts of the text three times before you answer a question. This will take you 20–30 minutes. Writing the answers should only take 20 minutes. This leaves 10–15 minutes for the translation.

Translation into English

The translation, worth 10 marks, is an exercise in accuracy and precision. The text for translation can come at any point in the text and is divided into five sense units, each worth 2 marks. For details of how this is marked, see page 11 of the Marking Instructions: http://www.sqa.org.uk/pastpapers/papers/instructions/2012/mi_H_German_Reading_2012.pdf .

To gain full marks in each section, you must ensure that you have

- translated every single word
- kept to the structure of the German
- used correct English grammar
- used the correct verb tense
- identified any comparative or superlative adjectives.

Read over everything you have written and double check that nothing has been left out. It is not difficult to score 2 marks in any section, but it is very easy to throw away marks. For detailed advice on the skill of translation, look at pages 5 and 6 of the 2012 External Assessment Report: http://www.sqa.org.uk/sqa/files_ccc/GermanHigherEAR2012.pdf.

Directed Writing

You should allow 40 minutes for this part of the exam. You are given a scenario, in English which you should read carefully.

You must include the information asked for in each of 6 bullet points. The total length of the piece should be 150–180 words, so a well-constructed response will have 6 roughly equal paragraphs of 25–30 words.

The opening two bullet points are predictable and are double bullet points; you **must** address both parts of the task, e.g. where you stayed **and** how you got on with the whole family. It is easy to exceed 30 words in these bullet points, but a good response should have no more words here than in the other four bullet points. Balance is important!

In bullet points 3–5, you might be asked to write about a day in a German school or a work experience placement. You are likely to be asked about an organised event in which you took part, how you spent your free time, what you did on the last night etc. The final bullet point will ask for an opinion or recommendation and you **must** read this carefully. It might ask about being in Germany at a certain time of year, and your answer must be specific to what is asked.

Content and balance are important. So is the quality of your writing in German. This exercise requires you to write in a past tense, probably the perfect tense, and you must have a sound knowledge of this tense and be able to use a variety of verbs.

If your verbs are correct, you are likely to score at least 9 marks. For a higher mark, focus on genders, cases, adjectives (with correct endings), adverbs and inverted word order. This will help you towards achieving 12 marks. For 15 marks, you should write complex sentences with subordinate clauses beginning with *obwohl, nachdem, weil* etc.

Check that you do not miss anything out. If you do, you will lose 2 marks. If you fail to address 3 of the bullet points, you will score 0.

Listening

In the Listening test, you will hear (twice) a recording of an interview of about 4 minutes. Before the first playing you have two minutes to study the questions. Read each question carefully and highlight the question word. This gives you a good idea about what you will hear. The questions are often translations of the questions within the interview.

You may make notes at any time, but make sure this does not stop you listening to the recording. If you hear a word you do not recognise, write it down so that you can work it out later. Sentences are not required but all the essential information is!

In the two minutes between playings, look over your responses to check that they answer the questions. During the second playing, focus on the **accuracy** of the answers you already have and the **information** you still have to gather.

At the end, check that your answers are clearly written and that you have crossed out any notes. The remaining 45 minutes of the exam are for the Personal Response writing task.

Personal Response Writing

You have to write 120–150 words, mainly in the present tense, on a subject closely related to the listening topic. You may also want to use the conditional tense (*ich würde…fahren*) or express your wishes by means of *ich möchte*. Read carefully the task set and respond appropriately to it. Do not include irrelevant information.

Once again, the verbs are critical, so make sure these are all correct. To gain a top mark, include complex sentences with subordinate clauses. Read over your response and carry out these checks:

- Do the verbs agree with the subject?
- Is the word order correct?
- Are the genders of nouns correct?
- Do you have the correct ending on the adjectives?
- Have you written at least 120 words?

And finally...

If you can tick off each of these, you can be satisfied that you have done your best. The 3 hours since the start of the exam are almost over and there is nothing more you can do other than await your exam results in August.

Good luck!

HIGHER

2009

[BLANK PAGE]

X060/301

NATIONAL
QUALIFICATIONS
2009

WEDNESDAY, 20 MAY
1.00 PM – 2.40 PM

GERMAN
HIGHER
Reading and
Directed Writing

45 marks are allocated to this paper. The value attached to each question is shown after each question.

You should spend approximately one hour on Section I and 40 minutes on Section II.

You may use a German dictionary.

SECTION I—READING

Read the whole of this newspaper article carefully and then answer **in English** the questions which follow it.

Three generations of a German family write about their experiences of summer. Grandmother Ingrid Dehnert (65) and mother Katrin Bredner (43) compare with daughter Carolin (17) how summer was then and what it is like now.

Von Limo zu Tequila Sunrise

Das, was die Menschen am Sommer genießen, scheint sich im Laufe der Zeit nicht geändert zu haben. Sonne, Wärme und Freizeit sind auch für diese drei Frauen die
5 absolut besten Dinge an der sommerlichen Jahreszeit. Wie man die freie Zeit jedoch nutzt, das hat sich mit jeder Generation stark verändert.

Ferienbeschäftigung

10 „Als ich noch jung war, machte ich in der Sommerzeit immer viel mit Freunden zusammen. Wir gingen viel baden, mussten aber immer laufen, da es noch keine Busse gab. Ich arbeitete nebenbei auch als
15 Kindermädchen und verdiente am Tag 50 Pfennige und eine Buttersemmel", berichtet Oma Ingrid Dehnert. „Wir haben auch immer die Touristen von der Fähre abgeholt und ihre Koffer in die Pensionen
20 gefahren. Wir sind aber nie in den Urlaub gefahren, weil wir nicht genug Geld hatten. Meine Mutter sagte oft zu uns Kindern: ‚Ich möchte so gerne einmal mit euch in die Berge fahren . . .!' Sie wollte uns immer die
25 Alpen zeigen."

In der Generation von Mutter Katrin Bredner war es schon anders: „Ich habe ab und zu in der Milchbar gearbeitet, bin sehr viel wandern gegangen, und manchmal sind
30 wir auch in den Urlaub an die Ostsee gefahren."

Tochter Carolin erzählt: „Heute gehen wir viel in die Disco, auf Open-Air-Konzerte, ins Kino und Döner, Pizza oder Eis essen."

35 ### Essen und Trinken

„Egal, wo wir hingegangen sind, wir haben unser Essen mitgenommen. Wenn wir das Geld hatten, haben wir eine Flasche Limonade gekauft, die wir uns geteilt
40 haben", erzählt Oma Ingrid. Die Getränke des Sommers haben sich im Laufe der Zeit stark geändert. Von Limonade bis Cola war es ein langer Weg. Heute stehen

Mixgetränke wie Tequila Sunrise oder Cosmopolitan auf der Getränkekarte. 45

Sommermode

Auch in Sachen Kleidung passierte ein großer Wandel. „Früher hatten wir noch selbst geschneiderte Sachen. Wir trugen in der Regel Kleider und Röcke. Außerdem 50 krempelten wir die Röcke hoch, um Miniröcke zu erhalten. Meine Lieblingsfarbe des Sommers war damals Rot", sagt die Großmutter.

„In unserer Zeit gab es schon Miniröcke, 55 aber auch kurze Hosen. Die Farbe des Sommers war damals Blau", so Katrin Bredner. Carolin Bredner weiß, wie es jetzt aussieht: „Heute sind viele Farben aktuell. Auch Streifen werden oft getragen", sagt sie. 60

Party und Feiern

Neben der Mode sind noch weitere Unterschiede festzustellen. Viele Jugendliche in der heutigen Zeit nutzen die Ferien, um richtig zu feiern. Daran war früher 65 nicht zu denken. In der Generation von Ingrid Dehnert waren die einzigen Feiermöglichkeiten Familienfeste, und selbst dann mussten die Kinder um Mitternacht zu Hause sein. Katrin Bredner dagegen lebt in 70 einer Generation, die in ihrer Jugend schon viel die Disco besuchte. Heute ist es am extremsten. „Wir gehen heute, wenn es klappt, jedes Wochenende in die Disco. Jugendliche besuchen auch Stadtfeste zum 75 Feiern", erklärt Carolin.

Musik und Sommerhits

Die spannendste Verwandlung passierte jedoch bei der Musik. Als Oma Ingrid noch jung war, wurden nur Wanderlieder 80 gesungen. Jedoch in der Generation von Katrin Bredner war das schon ganz anders. Die Jugendlichen nahmen ihre eigenen Stimmen und viel Musik mit einem Kassettenrekorder auf und hörten sich diese 85 an. Heute kommt nahezu kein Jugendlicher ohne MP3-Player oder I-Pod aus.

Fazit

90 Zum Schluss sollen die drei Frauen den Satz „Ich habe den Sommer in meiner Jugend genossen, weil . . .“ fortsetzen.

„. . . weil man Freizeit hat und die Sonne und die Ruhe genießen kann“, antwortet Carolin Bredner. Ihre Mutter Katrin sagt: „. . . weil mir die Sonne sehr wichtig war und 95 man sich entspannen konnte.“ Die Antwort von Oma Ingrid ist jedoch die, die am meisten fasziniert. „Wir waren frei“, sagt sie.

QUESTIONS

Marks

1. (a) Across the three generations, what has **not** changed over the years?   **1**

    (b) What has changed a great deal?   **1**

2. Read lines 9–34.

    (a) What does grandmother Ingrid Dehnert say about going swimming with friends in summer, when she was young?   **1**

    (b) Apart from child-minding, what did she do to earn money?   **2**

    (c) How did Katrin Bredner spend her holidays?   **2**

3. Read lines 35–45.

    In grandmother Ingrid's day, what did they do for food and drink, when they went out?   **2**

4. Now read lines 46–60.

    (a) What sort of clothes did grandmother Ingrid's generation wear in the summer?   **1**

    (b) What does Katrin say about clothes in her day?   **1**

    (c) What do today's young people wear?   **1**

5. Read lines 61–76.

    (a) What are you told about parties, when Ingrid was young?   **2**

    (b) How do the young people of today like to celebrate?   **2**

6. Read lines 77–87.

    What changes in music took place between Oma Ingrid's and Katrin Bredner's generation?   **2**

7. Read lines 88–98.

    Why did Katrin enjoy summers, when she was a girl?   **2**

    (20)

    = 20 marks

8. Translate into English:

    „Wir sind aber . . . uns immer die Alpen zeigen.“ (lines 20–25)   **10**

    (30)

[Turn over for SECTION II on *Page four*

SECTION II—DIRECTED WRITING

Marks

You have travelled to Germany to spend three months working in a town there.

When you return to Scotland, you have to write a report **in German** for the languages department in your school/college.

You must include the following information and **you should try to add** other relevant details:

*   how you travelled to Germany **and** what the town was like

*   where your accommodation was situated **and** what it was like

*   what your job involved **and** how you got on with the people you worked with

*   what you did in your spare time to experience the country/culture

*   what you did on your last night before coming home

*   why you would/would not recommend working in Germany to others.

Your report should be 150 – 180 words in length.

Marks will be deducted for any area of information that is omitted. (15)

[END OF QUESTION PAPER]

X060/303

NATIONAL
QUALIFICATIONS
2009

WEDNESDAY, 20 MAY
3.00 PM – 4.00 PM

GERMAN
HIGHER
Listening Transcript

This paper must not be seen by any candidate.

The material overleaf is provided for use in an emergency only (eg the recording or equipment proving faulty) or where permission has been given in advance by SQA for the material to be read to candidates with additional support needs. The material must be read exactly as printed.

Instructions to reader(s):

The dialogue below should be read in approximately 3½ minutes. On completion of the first reading, pause for two minutes, then read the dialogue a second time.

Where special arrangements have been agreed in advance to allow the reading of the material, those sections marked **(m)** should be read by a male speaker and those marked **(f)** by a female.

Candidates have two minutes to study the questions before the transcript is read.

Meike, a 20 year-old German from Markersdorf near Görlitz in Saxony, talks about getting a training place.

(m)   Meike, wo kommst du her und wo wohnst du jetzt?

(f)   Ich komme aus Markersdorf. Das ist eine Gemeinde in Sachsen mit etwa 4.500 Einwohnern. Jetzt wohne ich in Hamburg, das ist eine Großstadt und liegt etwa 500 km von Görlitz entfernt.

(m)   Warum bist du nach Hamburg gezogen?

(f)   Hier in Görlitz gibt es nur relativ wenige Ausbildungsplätze für die vielen Schüler. Für uns gibt es nur eine einzige Alternative. Wir müssen unsere Stadt, Eltern und Freunde verlassen, um in einer anderen Stadt einen Ausbildungsplatz zu bekommen. Deswegen bin ich nach Hamburg gezogen.

(m)   Wie war das am Anfang?

(f)   Nicht so einfach. Natürlich habe ich meine Freunde, meine Familie und meine Umgebung vermisst. Am Anfang kennt man ja niemanden. Mittlerweile habe ich schon viele Freunde gefunden.

(m)   Gibt es Vorteile, wenn man weit weg von zu Hause wohnt?

(f)   Selbstverständlich! Man kann Freunde mit nach Hause bringen - egal wie spät es ist. Und am Wochenende kann man solange schlafen, wie man will.

(m)   Gibt es auch Nachteile?

(f)   Na klar. Man muss alles selbst machen. Das bedeutet, man muss selbst einkaufen, selbst putzen und sich sein Geld einteilen, damit es bis zum Ende des Monats reicht.

(m)   Wolltest du von zu Hause wegziehen?

(f)   Eigentlich, ja. Für mich war es eine gute Entscheidung, fortzugehen. Im Vergleich zu meinen alten Klassenkameraden und Freunden, die in Görlitz arbeiten, verdiene ich auch mehr Geld.

(m)   Wie hast du diese Ausbildungsstelle in Hamburg bekommen?

(f)   Eigentlich nur durch Zufall! Ein Arbeitskollege ist krank geworden und ich habe seinen Platz bekommen. Ich war recht froh, diese Stelle in Hamburg zu bekommen, weil ich in Norddeutschland leben wollte.

(m)   Wie ist es mit dem Umzug nach Hamburg gelaufen?

(f)   Ich hatte das Glück, dass meine Eltern mich beim Umzug sehr unterstützt haben. Sie haben mir sehr viel geholfen. Sie sind mit mir zusammen nach Hamburg gefahren und wir haben eine Wohnung gesucht. Innerhalb von drei Tagen haben sie mit mir alles für die Wohnung gekauft.

(m) **Ist es wirklich ein großer Unterschied, ob man in Hamburg oder in Görlitz lebt?**

(f) Ja, das sowieso. Hamburg ist nicht nur sehr viel größer, die Einwohner sprechen auch einen anderen Dialekt.

(m) **Fährst du noch oft nach Görlitz?**

(f) Nicht so oft. Aber ich bin froh, wenn ich mal wieder zu Hause bin, weil ich dann meine alten Freunde treffen kann.

(m) **War es für dich ein sehr großer Schritt von zu Hause auszuziehen?**

(f) Sicher. Seitdem ich in Hamburg wohne, bin ich auf jeden Fall selbstständiger geworden und vielleicht sogar ein Stück erwachsener.

[END OF TRANSCRIPT]

[BLANK PAGE]

FOR OFFICIAL USE

Examiner's Marks	
A	
B	

Total Mark

X060/302

NATIONAL
QUALIFICATIONS
2009

WEDNESDAY, 20 MAY
3.00 PM – 4.00 PM

GERMAN
HIGHER
Listening/Writing

Fill in these boxes and read what is printed below.

Full name of centre

Town

Forename(s)

Surname

Date of birth

Day Month Year   Scottish candidate number   Number of seat

Do not open this paper until told to do so.

Answer Section A **in English** and Section B **in German**.

Section A

Listen carefully to the recording with a view to answering, **in English**, the questions printed in this answer book. Write your answers **clearly and legibly** in the spaces provided after each question.

You will have 2 minutes to study the questions before hearing the dialogue for the first time.

The dialogue will be played **twice**, with an interval of 2 minutes between the two playings.

You may make notes at any time but only in this answer book. **Score out any notes before you hand in the book.**

Move on to Section B when you have completed Section A: you will **not** be told when to do this.

Section B

Do not write your response in this book: **use the 4 page lined answer sheet**.

You will be told to insert the answer sheet inside this book before handing in your work.

You may consult a German dictionary at any time during **both** sections.

Before leaving the examination room you must give this book to the invigilator. If you do not, you may lose all the marks for this paper.

SA X060/302 6/6020

Section A

Marks

Meike, a 20 year-old German from Markersdorf near Görlitz in Saxony, talks about getting a training place.

1.   How many people live in Markersdorf?   **1 point**

2.   (*a*) What does Meike say about the number of training places in Görlitz?   **1 point**

     (*b*) What is the only alternative the young people have?   **1 point**

3.   At the beginning, how did she find living in Hamburg?   **2 points**

4.   What are the advantages of living far away from home?   **2 points**

5.   What are the disadvantages?   **3 points**

6.   Why does she feel that moving away was a good decision?   **1 point**

Marks

7. (*a*) How did Meike get this training place?   **1 point**

   (*b*) Why was she pleased?   **1 point**

8. How did her parents help her with the move to Hamburg?   **3 points**

9. What are the **two** differences between Hamburg and Görlitz?   **2 points**

10. Why does she like to go back to Görlitz?   **1 point**

11. How has she changed since leaving home?   **1 point**

**(20 points)
= 20 marks**

[Turn over for Section B on *Page four*

Marks

Section B

Was meinst du, was sind die Vorteile und Nachteile von deinem Wohnort? Willst du lieber bei den Eltern wohnen oder von Zuhause ausziehen?

Schreibe 120 – 150 Worte zu diesen Fragen!

10

(30)

USE THE 4 PAGE LINED ANSWER SHEET FOR YOUR ANSWER TO SECTION B

[END OF QUESTION PAPER]

[BLANK PAGE]

[BLANK PAGE]

X060/301

NATIONAL
QUALIFICATIONS
2010

WEDNESDAY, 19 MAY
1.00 PM – 2.40 PM

GERMAN
HIGHER
Reading and
Directed Writing

45 marks are allocated to this paper. The value attached to each question is shown after each question.

You should spend approximately one hour on Section I and 40 minutes on Section II.

You may use a German dictionary.

SECTION I—READING

Read the whole of this newspaper article carefully and then answer **in English** the questions which follow it.

Annette leaves Germany to live in Cape Town in South Africa.

Neue Heimat

Von Deutschland nach Südafrika—am Anfang will Annette einfach nur raus aus ihrem Dorf. Irgendwohin. „Ich wollte dahin, wo mich niemand kennt", sagt
5 Annette. „Als Pastorentochter kannst du dich nicht betrinken", sagt sie. „Zumindest nicht, wenn du deinen Eltern nicht peinlich sein möchtest." Annette versteht sich nämlich gut mit ihnen.

10 Sie hat keine Lust auf schlaue Tipps, auf Leute, die ihr erzählen, wie es woanders ist. Sie sucht im Internet, besorgt sich Broschüren, sammelt Informationen über die Arbeit als Au-pair. Und findet dabei eine
15 Vermittlung aus *Kapstadt*: Ein Jahr Südafrika, das ist es!

Aber es geht noch um anderes: „Ich wollte wissen: Wie komme ich allein klar? Wo gehöre ich hin? Wer bin ich?", sagt Annette.
20 Doch die Eltern legen ihr Veto ein. Sie machen sich Sorgen. *Kapstadt*—„Da kann man doch als Frau nicht auf die Straße gehen". Aber je größer der Widerstand, desto entschlossener ist Annette.

25 Sie erinnert sich genau daran, wie sie mit ihren Eltern im Wohnzimmer sitzt: diskutiert, erklärt, protestiert. Schließlich zieht sie den Joker: „Ihr habt mir meine Selbständigkeit beigebracht. Und jetzt wollt
30 ihr mir eine so wichtige Entscheidung aus den Händen nehmen? Ich glaube nicht, dass das richtig ist", sagt sie. Die Eltern schauen sich an. Zehn lange Sekunden. Und unterschreiben das Formular, ohne ein Wort
35 zu sagen. Ihre Tochter hat Recht.

Drei Tage nach dem Abi-Ball geht es los. Als Annette am Flughafen durch die Zollabfertigung geht, dreht sie sich zu ihrer Familie um, winkt und verschwindet. „Jetzt
40 ist sie für immer aus dem Haus", denkt ihr Vater, „die kommt nicht mehr als meine kleine Tochter zurück."

Als sie in *Kapstadt* ankommt, geht es zu den Gasteltern. Alles läuft nach Plan: Die Familie ist nett, mit den beiden Kindern 45 kommt sie klar. Annette macht Frühstück, bringt die Kinder zur Schule. Sie genießt das Leben, geht ins Fitness-Studio, legt sich in die Sonne und liest viel. Nachmittags macht sie den Kindern einen Imbiss und 50 spielt mit ihnen, bis die Eltern kommen. Annette ist froh, weil sie Ruhe hat.

Und dann kommt Karel. Ihr Gastvater hatte seinen Kollegen Karel gebeten, Annette abends in die Clubs mitzunehmen, 55 damit sie das junge *Kapstadt* kennen lernt und sich nicht langweilt. Karel und sie verstehen sich. Sehr sogar. Genau 18 Tage nach dem Kennenlernen will Annette von Karel wissen, was los ist. Ein Kuss und eine 60 Entscheidung. Annette ist erst seit vier Monaten in *Kapstadt*, aber sie weiß: Ich will bleiben. Hier studieren, mit Karel leben.

Im April 2008, kurz vor Ende des Au-pair-Jahres, fliegen Annettes Vater und ihr älterer 65 Bruder nach *Kapstadt*. Sie wollen sich anschauen, wie Annette lebt und wer eigentlich dieser Kerl ist, der alles durcheinander bringt. Karel und Annette sind nervös. Aber die Männer verstehen sich. 70 Alles passt.

Zwei Monate später muss Annette nach Deutschland zurück, um sich für den Studienplatz in *Kapstadt* zu bewerben. Es gibt viele Probleme mit dem Visum, aber ein 75 halbes Jahr später geht der Antrag endlich durch.

Karel kommt über Weihnachten und Silvester nach Deutschland. Als es Zeit für den Rückflug ist, freut sich Annette und ist 80 zugleich sehr traurig. „Ich weiß, dass es für meine Familie schwer ist, aber es ist bestimmt die richtige Entscheidung für mich. Ich wünsche mir nur, dass meine

85 Eltern mich verstehen." Das tun sie, aber natürlich vermissen sie die Tochter, jeden Sonntagabend hängen sie am Telefon.

Letztes Jahr Silvester feierten sie die Hochzeit in Südafrika. Annettes Familie kam 90 eingeflogen. Freunde aus Deutschland feierten fröhlich mit den neuen aus *Kapstadt*.

Es war ein richtig tolles Fest.

Und nun? Wollen beide für immer in *Kapstadt* bleiben? Oder steht irgendwann wieder Deutschland auf dem Lebensplan? 95 „Mal sehen", sagt Annette und grinst. „Wir lassen das offen." Keine Pläne mehr. Sondern: das Leben genießen. Jetzt.

QUESTIONS

Marks

1. Why did Annette first want to leave her village? **1**

2. Read lines 10–24.

    (*a*) Whose advice was she not interested in? **1**

    (*b*) How did her parents react to her idea of going to Cape Town? **2**

3. Read lines 25–35.

    What was the joker she played? **2**

4. Now read lines 36–42.

    What were her father's thoughts, as she passed through customs at the airport? **2**

5. Read lines 43–52.

    (*a*) What was Annette's morning routine in Cape Town? Write **four** things. **2**

    (*b*) What **two** tasks did she have in the afternoons? **2**

6. Read lines 53–63.

    (*a*) How did Annette come to meet Karel? **2**

    (*b*) What did she realise four months later? **1**

7. Read lines 64–71.

    Why did Annette's father and brother fly out to Cape Town in April 2008? **2**

8. Read lines 72–77.

    Why did Annette have to go back to Germany two months later? **1**

9. Read lines 88–98.

    Now that Annette and Karel are married, what are their thoughts for the future? **2**

    (20)

10. Translate into English:

    „Karel kommt . . . die richtige Entscheidung für mich." (lines 78–84) **10**

    (30)

[Turn over for SECTION II on *Page four*

Marks

SECTION II—DIRECTED WRITING

A German pupil is spending a year at your school/college in Scotland. He/she invited you to go back with him/her to Germany at Easter to spend two weeks with his/her family.

When you return to Scotland, you write **in German** for the languages page of your school/college website.

You must include the following information and **you should try to add** other relevant details:

*   how the two of you travelled to Germany **and** what the journey was like

*   what the town was like **and** what you thought of the family home

*   what you did to help around the home, while you were in Germany

*   what you and your German friend did in the afternoons and evenings

*   what you liked most/least about the family and the other people you met

*   why you would/would not recommend being in Germany just before your Higher exams.

(15)

Your report should be 150 – 180 words in length.

Marks will be deducted for any area of information that is omitted.

[END OF QUESTION PAPER]

X060/303

NATIONAL
QUALIFICATIONS
2010

WEDNESDAY, 19 MAY
3.00 PM – 4.00 PM

GERMAN
HIGHER
Listening Transcript

This paper must not be seen by any candidate.

The material overleaf is provided for use in an emergency only (eg the recording or equipment proving faulty) or where permission has been given in advance by SQA for the material to be read to candidates with additional support needs. The material must be read exactly as printed.

Instructions to reader(s):

The dialogue below should be read in approximately 3½ minutes. On completion of the first reading, pause for two minutes, then read the dialogue a second time.

Where special arrangements have been agreed in advance to allow the reading of the material, those sections marked **(m)** should be read by a male speaker and those marked **(f)** by a female.

Candidates have two minutes to study the questions before the transcript is read.

Rica, a German girl, talks about getting ready to go to the USA as an exchange student.

(m)   **Rica, du fliegst im August in die USA. Seit wann laufen die Vorbereitungen für diese Reise?**

(f)   Seit fast einem Jahr. Im Juli 2009 habe ich mich beim Rotary-Club Freital beworben, der diesen Austausch zum Teil finanziert. Nach sechs Wochen habe ich die nötigen Formulare bekommen, um mich anzumelden. Ich musste den Flug buchen und das Visum beantragen.

(m)   **Was musst du aus deiner eigenen Tasche bezahlen?**

(f)   Den Flug und die Versicherungen müssen wir bezahlen. Ich habe einen Teilzeitjob und habe etwas gespart, den Rest bezahlen meine Eltern.

(m)   **Warum ist dein Ziel die USA?**

(f)   Wir hatten hier eine Cousine aus den Staaten zu Besuch. Sie hat uns viel über die USA erzählt. Das weckte bei mir das Interesse an dem Land. Aber ich wäre auch in jedes andere Land gegangen. Ich will unbedingt richtig Englisch sprechen lernen.

(m)   **Nun ist es dein Wunschland geworden und du willst an einer Highschool lernen. Was begeistert dich so daran?**

(f)   Man hört immer so viel davon. Ich will mal sehen, ob dort wirklich alles so ist, wie man es in den Filmen sieht. Ob die Schule in Amerika mehr Spaß macht, als bei uns in Deutschland.

(m)   **Dich interessiert nur die Highschool?**

(f)   Nein, auch die Landschaft, die kulturellen Unterschiede und die vielen verschiedenen Aspekte des Landes.

(m)   **Wohin fliegst du genau?**

(f)   Nach Algonquin. Diese Kleinstadt liegt im Staat Illinois und ist ungefähr eine Autostunde von Chicago entfernt. Das Haus meiner Gastfamilie liegt direkt an einem Fluss.

(m)   **Wie lange wirst du weg sein?**

(f)   Elf Monate. Im August geht es los und im Juli nächsten Jahres komme ich wieder.

(m)   **Was sagen deine Freunde und deine Familie zu deinem Austauschjahr?**

(f)   Meine Mutter freut sich für mich. Aber es wird schwer für sie sein, wenn ich weg bin. Meine Freunde finden es gut, dass ich diese Möglichkeit habe.

(m)   Was musst du auf jeden Fall in den Koffer packen?

(f)   Fotos von meiner Familie und meinen Freunden. Erinnerungsstücke von meiner besten Freundin. Die Klaviernoten, damit ich das Spielen nicht verlerne und deutsche Rezepte von der Oma, darauf kann ich nicht verzichten.

(m)   Die USA bietet viele Sehenswürdigkeiten. Was willst du nicht verpassen?

(f)   Auf jeden Fall Chicago. Den Searstower—eines der größten Gebäude der Welt. Und wenn es klappt, fahre ich auch nach New York. Aber das ist ja schon ein ganzes Stück entfernt von Algonquin.

(m)   Was erhoffst du dir von diesem Auslandsjahr?

(f)   Ich hoffe, meine Englischkenntnisse verbessern zu können. Außerdem hoffe ich, dass ich nach diesem Jahr selbstbewusster und selbstständiger sein werde.

[END OF TRANSCRIPT]

[BLANK PAGE]

FOR OFFICIAL USE

Examiner's Marks	
A	
B	

Total Mark

X060/302

NATIONAL QUALIFICATIONS 2010

WEDNESDAY, 19 MAY 3.00 PM – 4.00 PM

GERMAN HIGHER
Listening/Writing

Fill in these boxes and read what is printed below.

Full name of centre

Town

Forename(s)

Surname

Date of birth

Day	Month	Year	Scottish candidate number	Number of seat

Do not open this paper until told to do so.

Answer Section A **in English** and Section B **in German**.

Section A

Listen carefully to the recording with a view to answering, **in English**, the questions printed in this answer book. Write your answers **clearly and legibly** in the spaces provided after each question.

You will have 2 minutes to study the questions before hearing the dialogue for the first time.

The dialogue will be played **twice**, with an interval of 2 minutes between the two playings.

You may make notes at any time but only in this answer book. **Score out any notes before you hand in the book.**

Move on to Section B when you have completed Section A: you will **not** be told when to do this.

Section B

Do not write your response in this book: **use the 4 page lined answer sheet**.

You will be told to insert the answer sheet inside this book before handing in your work.

You may consult a German dictionary at any time during **both** sections.

Before leaving the examination room you must give this book to the Invigilator. If you do not, you may lose all the marks for this paper.

SA X060/302 6/5310

Marks

Section A

Rica, a German girl, talks about getting ready to go to the USA as an exchange student.

1. (*a*) When did Rica first apply to the Rotary Club in Freital?   1

   (*b*) How long was it before she received the forms she needed?   1

2. Where is Rica getting the money from to pay for the flight and insurance?   2

3. Why did Rica choose to go to the United States rather than another English-speaking country?   2

4. What attracts Rica to go and study at an American high school?   2

5. Apart from the high school, what interests her? Mention **two** things.   2

6. Where in Illinois is Algonquin?   1

Marks

7. How long will Rica be away in America?   **1**

8. (*a*) How is Rica's mother going to feel about her going away to America?   **2**

    (*b*) What do her friends think about it?   **1**

9. Give details of the **three** things, other than photos, that Rica is taking with her.   **3**

10. Why might she not be able to go to New York while she is in America?   **1**

11. She sees this year as a chance to improve her English. Mention **one** other thing she would like to gain from the year.   **1**

(20)

[Turn over for Section B on *Page four*

Marks

Section B

Was meinst du, möchtest du ein Jahr in einem anderen Land verbringen? Wohin würdest du gehen? Warum?

Schreibe 120 – 150 Worte zu diesen Fragen!

10

(30)

USE THE 4 PAGE LINED ANSWER SHEET FOR YOUR ANSWER TO SECTION B

[END OF QUESTION PAPER]

[BLANK PAGE]

X060/301

NATIONAL QUALIFICATIONS 2011

THURSDAY, 19 MAY 1.00 PM – 2.40 PM

GERMAN
HIGHER
Reading and Directed Writing

45 marks are allocated to this paper. The value attached to each question is shown after each question.

You should spend approximately one hour on Section I and 40 minutes on Section II.

You may use a German dictionary.

SECTION I—READING

Read the whole of this newspaper article carefully and then answer **in English** the questions which follow it.

Christine Siefer is working during the main tourist season on the small East Friesian island of Juist, where no cars are allowed.

Hinter den Kulissen des Tourismus

Es ist ein typischer sommerlicher Strandtag auf der Ferieninsel *Juist*. Die Urlauber sonnen sich auf dem Platz vor dem *Café Kunststück*. Familien, die gerade vom Strand
5 kommen, gönnen sich ein kühles Getränk und ihren Kindern ein Eis. Mittendrin bin ich, als Kellnerin auf der schönsten Sandbank der Welt.

Ich fühlte mich schon nach wenigen Tagen
10 fast als Insider, die hinter die Kulissen einer Traumwelt schauen darf. Ich habe ein Zimmer in einem Haus, wo auch viele andere Helfer der großen Hotels wohnen. Die Stimmen, die durch die Hinterhöfe schallen,
15 gehören den Menschen, die die Insel als Urlaubsort funktionieren lassen, vom polnischen Zimmermädchen bis hin zum Hotelbesitzer, dessen Familie für den Rest des Jahres von der Arbeit und dem Verdienst
20 der Sommermonate lebt. Die Insel ist nämlich nur 17 Kilometer lang und wenige hundert Meter breit. Ausser in der Urlaubssaison gibt es hier nicht viel Arbeit. Die Kinder müssen auf dem Festland aufs
25 Gymnasium gehen, und die medizinische Versorgung hängt im Notfall von einem Hubschrauber ab.

Das alles interessiert die Urlauber überhaupt nicht. Ihr Ziel ist die Erholung
30 und Entspannung. Dazu tragen der lange weiße Sandstrand und die gute Meeresluft ohne Autoabgase bei.

In meiner ersten Woche war ich die einzige Aushilfskraft im Café, und ich bemerkte bei
35 meinen abendlichen Spaziergängen auf der Promenade ein mir bisher völlig fremdes Gefühl: Einsamkeit. Glücklicherweise folgte bald eine Kollegin im gleichen Alter, und ich fand schnell heraus, dass viele auswärtige
40 Jugendliche auf der Insel arbeiten. So lernte sogar ein Ausgehmuffel wie ich das Nachtleben der Insel kennen. Beim

Ausgehen am Abend überraschte es mich sehr, dass die Inselbewohner die gleichen Bars und Kneipen aufsuchen wie die 45 Urlauber. Dort treffen sich dann alle—Bewohner, Besucher und Aushilfskräfte.

Als die Ferien anfingen, blieb das Café zwölf Stunden täglich geöffnet. Von einem Tag auf den anderen war die Insel rappelvoll. 50 Fahrräder, Ziehkoffer und Pferdekutschen, wohin das Auge blickte. Wenn es dann plötzlich mal ein Schauer gibt, wird das Café zum Zufluchtsort Nummer eins. <u>Für uns bedeutet das: Hektik. Bestellungen 55 aufnehmen und servieren, nebenbei den Spülberg in Zaum halten und zwischendurch Geschenke aus dem Souvenirladen einpacken—nach solchen Tagen bin ich abends todmüde ins Bett gefallen.</u> 60

Inzwischen kann ich ein Tablett in der einen und Kuchenteller in der anderen Hand transportieren. In den ersten Wochen sind mir auch manchmal Tassen und Gläser vom Tablett gefallen. Fehler, die die Gäste 65 betrafen, waren mir peinlicher. Ich wollte an einem Tisch kassieren, habe aber nicht auf die Rechnung geschaut. Die Dame stellte sachlich fest, dass sie keine elf Weißbiere getrunken habe und hielt mir den Bon unter 70 die Nase. Ich hatte die Tischnummer verwechselt.

Sehr anstrengend war der Tag, an dem abends eine Rockband auf dem Kurplatz auftrat und die gesamte Insel vor dem Café 75 zusammentraf. Unsere Sitzplätze waren begehrt, und eine Stunde nach der offiziellen Schließung servierten wir weiter. Die meisten Konzertbesucher hatten wenig Verständnis dafür, dass wir endlich schließen wollten. 80 Viele Urlauber verstehen nicht, dass sich eine Servicekraft nach zwölfstündigem Arbeitstag nach dem Feierabend sehnt.

Dennoch: Gerade den Kontakt mit den
85 Gästen nehme ich als die schönste Erfahrung
mit nach Hause. Es ist ein unglaublich gutes
Gefühl, wenn Familien immer wieder ins
Café kommen, ich ihre Bestellung nach
einiger Zeit schon erraten kann und sich
90 nette Gespräche ergeben. Diese positiven

Begegnungen sind häufig und helfen mir,
auch <u>den</u> Feriengästen freundlich zu
begegnen, die keine zehn Minuten auf ihren
Kaffee warten können. Ich werde nie
verstehen können, wie sie zwischen Strand 95
und Hotel diesen Stress aufbauen können.

QUESTIONS

Marks

1. Describe what holiday-makers do on a typical summer's day on the island of Juist.   **3**

2. Read lines 9–27.

   (*a*) With whom does Christine share her accommodation?   **1**

   (*b*) What do you learn about the island of Juist and life there when the summer season is over?   **4**

3. Read lines 28–32.

   What **two** features help holiday-makers relax and recuperate?   **2**

4. Now read lines 33–47.

   (*a*) Why did Christine feel lonely at first?   **1**

   (*b*) How did this change?   **1**

   (*c*) What surprised Christine, when she started to visit the bars and pubs on the island?   **1**

5. Read lines 61–72.

   (*a*) What kind of unfortunate accident did she have in the first weeks of her job?   **1**

   (*b*) What embarrassing mistake did Christine make with one customer?   **1**

6. Read lines 73–83.

   What are Christine's complaints about the people who attended the concert in front of the café?   **2**

7. Read lines 84–96.

   (*a*) What gives Christine a really good feeling, when families keep coming back to the café?   **2**

   (*b*) Which customers do these positive experiences help her to cope with?   **1**

     (20)

8. Translate into English:

   „Für uns . . . ins Bett gefallen." (lines 54–60)   **10**

     (30)

[Turn over for SECTION II on *Page four*

Marks

SECTION II—DIRECTED WRITING

Last October you were invited to travel with a group from your local area to Bavaria to take part in a youth debate together with other young people from Germany and Austria. The debate was about smoking in cafés and restaurants.

When you return to Scotland, you write **in German** for the languages page of your school/college website.

You must include the following information and **you should try to add** other relevant details:

* how your group travelled to Germany **and** what you did during the journey

* what your host family were like **and** what their home was like

* how you got on with the other young people from Germany and Austria

* what you all did in the free time you had

* what you said in the debate and how the debate went

* why you would/would not recommend taking part in an international event like this.   **(15)**

Your report should be 150 – 180 words in length.

Marks will be deducted for any area of information that is omitted.

[END OF QUESTION PAPER]

X060/303

NATIONAL
QUALIFICATIONS
2011

THURSDAY, 19 MAY
3.00 PM – 4.00 PM

GERMAN
HIGHER
Listening Transcript

This paper must not be seen by any candidate.

The material overleaf is provided for use in an emergency only (eg the recording or equipment proving faulty) or where permission has been given in advance by SQA for the material to be read to candidates with additional support needs. The material must be read exactly as printed.

> **Instructions to reader(s):**
>
> The dialogue below should be read in approximately 4½ minutes. On completion of the first reading, pause for two minutes, then read the dialogue a second time.
>
> Where special arrangements have been agreed in advance to allow the reading of the material, those sections marked **(m)** should be read by a male speaker and those marked **(f)** by a female.
>
> **Candidates have two minutes to study the questions before the transcript is read.**

Alexandra, a German girl, is spending eight months in Scotland.

(m) **Wo wohnst du hier in Schottland?**

(f) Ich wohne in einem kleinen Dorf in Nordostschottland bei einer sehr netten Familie. Meine Eltern und ich hatten von Anfang an ein gutes Gefühl mit der Familie. Ich fühle mich sehr wohl bei der Familie und bin sehr dankbar hier zu sein. Rachel, die Tochter der Familie, ist in der gleichen Klasse hier wie ich.

(m) **Warum wolltest du nach Schottland kommen und hier eine Schule besuchen?**

(f) Ich habe einen Freund, der vor zwei Jahren in Schottland war. In der 11. Klasse in Deutschland gehen viele Schüler ins Ausland. Das Hauptziel für mich nach Schottland zu kommen war es, dass ich Englisch fließend sprechen kann.

(m) **Du bist ja Einzelkind. Wie findest du das?**

(f) Ja, das bin ich. Ich habe keine Brüder oder Schwestern, mit denen ich etwas teilen muss, und das finde ich gut so. Ich kriege die volle Aufmerksamkeit meiner Eltern und das genieße ich sehr.

(m) **Was ist für dich der größte Vorteil des Lebens als Einzelkind?**

(f) Ich bin ja eine ruhige Person, und ich finde es gut, wenn es ruhig bei uns zuhause ist. Ich bin daran gewöhnt, Zeit alleine zu verbringen.

(m) **Hier lebst du in einer Großfamilie. Was sind die Unterschiede?**

(f) Hier in einer Großfamilie zu leben ist ganz anders. Man muss teilen, und es herrscht ein regelrechter Wettbewerb um das Essen—jeder nimmt gleich am Anfang drei Stücke Pizza auf den Teller.

(m) **Wie ist es mit dem Bad, wenn ihr so viele in der Familie seid?**

(f) Wir mussten erstmal darüber sprechen, wann man ins Bad kann. Wir haben es aber hier gut, weil es mehrere Badezimmer gibt.

(m) **Verbringst du Zeit mit deiner Gastfamilie?**

(f) Meine Familie hier ist sehr unternehmungslustig. Sie haben viele Familienfreunde, die oft vorbei kommen, und dann ist das Haus voller Menschen. Manchmal gehen wir auch die Freunde besuchen und verbringen Abende und Nächte, in denen wir Karaoke singen und viel Spass haben. Wir sind zusammen auch schon öfters nach Inverness gegangen, um einzukaufen. Das hat mir auch Spass gemacht.

(m) **Was hat dich hier am meisten überrascht?**

(f) Ich fand es erstaunlich, dass die Schotten im allgemeinen so nett sind. Ich habe es nicht schwer gefunden, mich mit Leuten schnell zu verstehen oder in der Schlange im Supermarkt einfach mal in Gespräche mit fremden Menschen zu kommen.

(m)   **Und wie wirst du dich fühlen, wenn du wieder zuhause in Deutschland bist?**

(f)   Ich werde natürlich anfangs froh sein, wieder alle meine Freunde zu sehen. Auf der anderen Seite jedoch werde ich mein Leben hier in Schottland schon sehr vermissen. Ich habe dann 8 Monate meines Lebens hier verbracht und mich sehr an den Alltag hier gewöhnt. Es wird seltsam sein, die Menschen hier nicht mehr jeden Tag zu sehen, und ich werde sie alle sehr vermissen.

[END OF TRANSCRIPT]

[BLANK PAGE]

FOR OFFICIAL USE

Examiner's Marks	
A	
B	

Total Mark

X060/302

NATIONAL QUALIFICATIONS 2011

THURSDAY, 19 MAY 3.00 PM – 4.00 PM

GERMAN HIGHER Listening/Writing

Fill in these boxes and read what is printed below.

Full name of centre

Town

Forename(s)

Surname

Date of birth

Day	Month	Year		Scottish candidate number		Number of seat

Do not open this paper until told to do so.

Answer Section A **in English** and Section B **in German**.

Section A

Listen carefully to the recording with a view to answering, **in English**, the questions printed in this answer book. Write your answers **clearly and legibly** in the spaces provided after each question.

You will have 2 minutes to study the questions before hearing the dialogue for the first time.

The dialogue will be played **twice**, with an interval of 2 minutes between the two playings.

You may make notes at any time but only in this answer book. **Score out any notes before you hand in the book.**

Move on to Section B when you have completed Section A: you will **not** be told when to do this.

Section B

Do not write your response in this book: **use the 4 page lined answer sheet**.

You will be told to insert the answer sheet inside this book before handing in your work.

You may consult a German dictionary at any time during **both** sections.

Before leaving the examination room you must give this book to the Invigilator. If you do not, you may lose all the marks for this paper.

SA X060/302 6/4610

Marks

Section A

Alexandra, a German girl, is spending eight months in Scotland.

1.   (*a*) Where in Scotland is Alexandra staying?   1

      (*b*) What does she say about the family she is staying with?   Mention
             three things.   3

2.   Why did she want to come to Scotland?   2

3.   What does she say about being an only child?   1

4.   What is the biggest advantage of life as an only child?   1

5.   What are the differences of living in a large family?   3

6.   With so many people in the house, what are the arrangements for the
      bathroom?   2

Marks

7. What shows that her Scottish family likes to do lots of things? Mention **three** things.

    3

8. What has surprised Alexandra most about the Scots? Mention **two** things.

    2

9. How is she going to feel, when she is back in Germany?

    2

    (20)

[Turn over for Section B on *Page four*

Marks

Section B

Bist du Einzelkind oder kommst du aus einer größeren Familie? Wie kommst du mit deiner Familie aus? Möchtest du das ändern? Warum?

Schreibe 120 – 150 Worte zu diesen Fragen! **10**

(30)

USE THE 4 PAGE LINED ANSWER SHEET FOR YOUR ANSWER TO SECTION B

[END OF QUESTION PAPER]

HIGHER

2012

[BLANK PAGE]

X060/12/01

| NATIONAL QUALIFICATIONS 2012 | TUESDAY, 22 MAY 1.00 PM – 2.40 PM | GERMAN HIGHER Reading and Directed Writing |

45 marks are allocated to this paper. The value attached to each question is shown after each question.

You should spend approximately one hour on Section I and 40 minutes on Section II.

You may use a German dictionary.

SECTION I—READING

Read the whole of this newspaper article carefully and then answer **in English** the questions which follow it.

Jillian and Danny left home in the US more than a year ago to see the world. They are now in Germany and are staying with Anja, the writer of the article, and her boyfriend in Cologne.

Wenn einer eine Reise tut . . .

Es fing alles im Jahr 2009 an, als mein Freund und ich für unseren Amerika-Urlaub eine Bleibe in *Washington DC* gesucht haben. Über das Internet haben
5 wir Jillian und Danny gefunden. Wir haben sie über die Internetseite von „Couchsurfing" kennen gelernt. Die beiden sind in unserem Alter und haben uns ihre Couch zur Verfügung gestellt.

10 Nach unserem zweitägigen Aufenthalt bei Jillian und Danny war schnell klar, dass die beiden uns auch besuchen kommen sollen. Schon damals spukte eine Idee in den Köpfen der beiden: Eine Reise um
15 die Welt, jeder mit einem Rucksack und dem Nötigsten ausgerüstet—zwei Paar Hosen, drei T-Shirts, Unterwäsche für ein paar Tage, Seife, Shampoo, Zahnbürste, Trinkflasche und Campingausrüstung.
20 Das Badetuch und die Kleidung sind aus Microfaser, schnell trocknend und wasseraufsaugend; alles ist praktisch, schnell waschbar und leicht. Denn das ist das Wichtigste: Alles muss leicht sein.

25 Die beiden haben keinen Zeitdruck auf ihrer Tour. Vor der Abreise haben sie ihren sicheren Job gekündigt. Die Idee ihrer Reise: sich durch nichts und niemanden beeinflussen lassen; einfach zwei Jahre lang
30 leben.

Die Idee dazu hatten die beiden schon früh. Seit dem Collegeabschluss haben sie gespart, um die Reise bezahlen zu können. Außerdem haben sie vor der Abreise
35 die Wohnung und das Auto verkauft, die wichtigsten Sachen bei den Eltern eingelagert, den Rest haben sie verschenkt. Als der Tag der Abreise näher rückte, kam auch die Anspannung und die Frage, ob
40 alles gut gehen wird. „Auf der einen Seite war ich traurig, meine Freunde und Familie zu verlassen, auf der anderen Seite habe ich mich gefreut, auf eine Weltreise zu gehen", erklärt Jillian.

45 Von ihrer Heimatstadt flogen sie zuerst nach Mexiko, anschließend nach Mittel- und Südamerika. „Wir haben dort viele Ziele eingeplant", erzählt Danny. „Die eigentliche Herausforderung ist es, mit Enttäuschungen fertig zu werden,
50 besonders wenn etwas nicht so ist, wie man es sich vorgestellt hat."

Nach ihrem neunmonatigen Aufenthalt in Südamerika flogen sie Ende November 2010 zurück nach Hause. „Für uns war
55 es billiger, erst nach Hause zu fliegen und von dort nach Südafrika zu fliegen als von Südamerika nach Südafrika", erklärt Danny. Nach Südafrika reisten sie weiter über Simbabwe, Uganda, und den Nahen
60 Osten nach Deutschland. Danach soll es über Russland nach Asien gehen.

Auf die Frage, was sie nach ihrer Weltreise machen wollen, schauen mich die beiden ratlos an. „Wir haben keine
65 Ahnung," gesteht Danny. Auch Jillian hat noch keine festen Pläne. Vielleicht noch mal studieren oder wieder in den Beruf. „Wir wissen auch noch nicht, in welcher Stadt oder in welchem Staat wir leben
70 werden", sagt Danny.

Eins wissen sie hingegen: Es soll nicht zurück ins alte Leben gehen. „Ich vermisse den Lebensstil, den wir aufgegeben haben, den Fitnessclub, eine gesunde
75 Ernährung, Wochenendausflüge. Aber ich möchte jetzt keinen Job, in dem ich von 9 bis 17 Uhr arbeite und Papier auf dem Schreibtisch herumschiebe", meint Danny. Auch Jillian vermisst die
80 alltäglichen Dinge, die ihr früher auf die Nerven gingen. Wäsche waschen, Essen

kochen, spülen—die tägliche Routine fehlt ihr. Aber sie möchte auch nicht missen, was sie alles erfahren und gelernt hat: „Unsere Beziehung ist anders geworden, viel enger, weil man die ganze Zeit zusammen ist", sagt sie. „In dieser Situation kann man nicht mehr vor den Launen des anderen fliehen, sondern muss damit umgehen. Man kann seine Gefühle nicht verstecken", klärt Jillian mich auf und lächelt Danny an. Schnell sind die vier Tage vorbei. Und wieder heißt es packen, eine Weiterreisemöglichkeit finden, Übernachtungen organisieren.

QUESTIONS

Marks

1. Read lines 1–9.

   (a) How did Anja come to meet Jillian and Danny?   1

   (b) What are you told about Jillian and Danny?   1

2. Read lines 10–24.

   Why have they chosen to take clothes and towels made of microfibres?

   Mention **four** things.   2

3. Read lines 25–30.

   (a) Why is there no time pressure on Jillian and Danny now?   1

   (b) What is the idea behind their trip? Mention **two** things.   2

4. Read lines 31–44.

   (a) What did they do with all their possessions, before they left America?   3

   (b) How did Jillian feel, just before they left?   2

5. Read lines 45–52.

   What is the most challenging aspect of the trip?   2

6. Read lines 53–62.

   Why did they go back home in November 2010?   1

7. Read lines 63–71.

   What are their thoughts and plans for after their world trip? Mention **two** things.   2

8. Read lines 72–96.

   (a) What **exactly** does Jillian say is different in their relationship?   1

   (b) What are the reasons for this? Mention **two** things.   2

      (20)

9. Translate into English:

   „Ich vermisse . . . auf die Nerven gingen. (lines 73–82)   10

      (30)

[Turn over for SECTION II on *Page four*

SECTION II—DIRECTED WRITING   *Marks*

Two years ago you hosted a German student for nine months and last year you were invited by the student's family to spend the entire summer with them; this included going on holiday with them.

When you return to Scotland, you write a report **in German** for the Languages page of your school/college website.

You must include the following information and **you should try to add** other relevant details:

- where in Germany the family live **and** whether you had ever been to Germany before

- what your host family were like **and** how you got on with them

- what you did to help out in the family home

- what you liked about a special outing you went on

- what you found to be different about going away on holiday with a family other than your own one

- whether or not you felt it was a good experience for you to be away from Scotland for such a long time.   **(15)**

Your report should be 150–180 words in length.

Marks will be deducted for any area of information that is omitted.

[END OF QUESTION PAPER]

X060/12/12

NATIONAL
QUALIFICATIONS
2012

TUESDAY, 22 MAY
3.00 PM – 4.00 PM

GERMAN
HIGHER
Listening Transcript

This paper must not be seen by any candidate.

The material overleaf is provided for use in an emergency only (eg the recording or equipment proving faulty) or where permission has been given in advance by SQA for the material to be read to candidates with additional support needs. The material must be read exactly as printed.

Instructions to reader(s):

The dialogue below should be read in approximately 4½ minutes. On completion of the first reading, pause for two minutes, then read the dialogue a second time.

Where special arrangements have been agreed in advance to allow the reading of the material, those sections marked **(m)** should be read by a male speaker and those marked **(f)** by a female speaker.

Candidates have two minutes to study the questions before the transcript is read.

Svenja, a German girl, recently spent a year in a school in Britain.

(m)   **In Deutschland wird viel über das Thema Schuluniform diskutiert, weil es bei euch normalerweise so was nicht gibt. Wie siehst du die Sache?**

(f)   Also, ich weiß, dass das Tragen dieser Uniformen in vielen Ländern etwas ganz typisches ist. In Großbritannien und auch in vielen anderen Ländern wie Australien und Neuseeland sind Schuluniformen auch heute noch Pflicht.

(m)   **Du hast neulich ein Jahr in Grossbritannien verbracht und bist dort zur Schule gegangen. Musstest du auch eine Schuluniform tragen?**

(f)   Ja, als Schülerin in England musste ich eine Schuluniform tragen und zwar einen knielangen dunkelblauen Rock, eine weiße Bluse, eine Krawatte und auch einen Blazer mit Schullogo.

(m)   **Hast du deine Schuluniform gerne angezogen?**

(f)   Ja, das hat mich nicht gestört, denn man hat immer die gleichen Sachen an. Man braucht nicht darüber nachzudenken, was man morgens anzieht. Aber bei anderen Mädchen gab es Probleme. Viele haben versucht, aus der Uniform ein individuelles Outfit zu machen.

(m)   **Wie haben sie das gemacht?**

(f)   Sie haben zum Beispiel ihre Röcke kürzer gemacht oder ihre Blazer mit Buttons dekoriert.

(m)   **Und hat es sonst noch Probleme mit der Uniform gegeben?**

(f)   Nicht mit der Uniform selbst, aber andere Schülerinnen haben ziemlich extreme Punkfrisuren getragen oder große Ohrringe.

(m)   **Haben teure Markenklamotten bei dir eine große Rolle gespielt?**

(f)   Na, klar. Wenn ich aus der Schule nach Hause gekommen bin, habe ich mich sofort umgezogen. Das mussten dann schon meine modischen Klamotten sein.

(m)   **Wie war es bei deinen Freundinnen in England?**

(f)   Sie haben sich auch umgezogen, als sie zu Hause angekommen sind. Das Problem aber ist, dass diese Markenklamotten teuer sind. Viele Eltern haben nicht das Geld für diese modischen Sachen.

(m)   **Aber mit der Schuluniform sieht man nicht mehr, wer reiche Eltern hat, oder?**

(f)   Doch, natürlich! Auch mit der Schuluniform sieht man, wer Geld hat und wer nicht. Das fängt schon damit an, dass man die Schuluniform selbst kaufen muss. Manche Schülerinnen müssen die Uniform von einer Schwester oder von einer Cousine nochmals tragen und können auch nicht so oft wechseln, weil sie nur zwei weiße Blusen haben.

(m) **Und die mit reichen Eltern?**

(f) Die Mädchen mit reichen Eltern haben vier oder fünf Blusen, die die Mutter jeden Tag bügelt. Da hat man natürlich Unterschiede gesehen. Und diese Unterschiede waren auch allen Leuten klar.

(m) **Was ist denn eigentlich passiert, wenn man die Uniform einfach nicht angezogen hat?**

(f) Das gab auf jeden Fall Stress. Man musste sich am nächsten Morgen bei der Schuldirektorin mit Uniform melden. Und wenn man die Uniform nicht anhatte, wurde man nach Hause geschickt, um sich umzuziehen.

(m) **Nach deinen Erfahrungen in England, glaubst du, dass man auch hier in Deutschland eine Schuluniform einführen sollte?**

(f) Das kommt darauf an. Die Schüler müssten damit einverstanden sein. Und sie müssten selber entscheiden, wie die Uniform aussieht. Zum Beispiel könnte man nur einen Schulpullover tragen, aber die andere Kleidung selbst wählen.

(m) **Gibt es schon Schulen in Deutschland, die eine Uniform haben?**

(f) Ja. In Hamburg gibt es eine Schule mit Uniform. Dort gibt es sogar je nach Jahreszeit verschiedene Uniformen.

[END OF TRANSCRIPT]

[BLANK PAGE]

FOR OFFICIAL USE

Examiner's Marks	
A	
B	

Total
Mark

X060/12/02

NATIONAL
QUALIFICATIONS
2012

TUESDAY, 22 MAY
3.00 PM – 4.00 PM

GERMAN
HIGHER
Listening/Writing

Fill in these boxes and read what is printed below.

Full name of centre

Town

Forename(s)

Surname

Date of birth

Day	Month	Year	Scottish candidate number	Number of seat

Do not open this paper until told to do so.

Answer Section A **in English** and Section B **in German**.

Section A

Listen carefully to the recording with a view to answering, **in English**, the questions printed in this answer book. Write your answers **clearly and legibly** in the spaces provided after each question.

You will have 2 minutes to study the questions before hearing the dialogue for the first time.

The dialogue will be played **twice**, with an interval of 2 minutes between the two playings.

You may make notes at any time but only in this answer book. **Score out any notes before you hand in the book.**

Move on to Section B when you have completed Section A: you will **not** be told when to do this.

Section B

Do not write your response in this book: **use the 4 page lined answer sheet**.

You will be told to insert the answer sheet inside this book before handing in your work.

You may consult a German dictionary at any time during **both** sections.

Before leaving the examination room you must give this book to the Invigilator. If you do not, you may lose all the marks for this paper.

Section A

Marks

Svenja, a German girl, recently spent a year in a school in Britain.

1. (*a*) What does Svenja say about the wearing of school uniform in many countries?

   1

   (*b*) In which **two** countries other than Britain are uniforms compulsory?

   1

2. When Svenja was in Britain, what uniform did she have to wear, apart from a tie and blazer? Mention **two** things.

   2

3. Why did wearing a school uniform not bother her?

   2

4. In what ways did some girls try to individualise their school uniforms?

   2

5. What steps did other girls take to show their individuality? Mention **one** thing.

   1

6. To what extent did designer clothes play a role in Svenja's life?

   1

Marks

7. What was **one** of the problems that Svenja was aware of with some families and designer clothes?   1

8. To what extent do school uniforms still show who has money and who does not? Mention **two** things.   2

9. What does Svenja say about the uniforms of pupils from better-off families?   2

10. What happened in her British school, if a pupil arrived at school not wearing uniform?   2

11. According to Svenja, what **two** conditions would have to be met, before a school uniform could be introduced in Germany?   2

12. What information does Svenja give about the uniform at one school in Hamburg?   1

(20)

[Turn over for Section B on *Page four*

Section B   *Marks*

Die Uniform in ihrer englischen Schule hat Svenja nicht gestört. Und du, was sind für dich die Vor- und Nachteile einer Schuluniform? Findest du es wichtig, die neueste Mode oder die richtige Marke zu tragen?

Schreibe 120 – 150 Worte zu diesen Fragen!   **10**

                                                                                            (30)

USE THE 4 PAGE LINED ANSWER SHEET FOR YOUR ANSWER TO SECTION B

[END OF QUESTION PAPER]

HIGHER

2013

[BLANK PAGE]

X060/12/01

NATIONAL
QUALIFICATIONS
2013

FRIDAY, 24 MAY
1.00 PM – 2.40 PM

GERMAN
HIGHER
Reading and
Directed Writing

45 marks are allocated to this paper. The value attached to each question is shown after each question.

You should spend approximately one hour on Section I and 40 minutes on Section II.

You may use a German dictionary.

SECTION I—READING

Read the whole of this newspaper article carefully and then answer **in English** the questions which follow it.

The Schneider family have 8 children—Joshua (12), Alexander (10), Max (9), Jonas and Anna (3), Jule and Emily (20 months) and Elias (5 months). This is a journalist's account of one day in the life of this large family.

Familie Schneider hat acht Kinder—Ein Tag mit einer Großfamilie

Drei bis vier Maschinen Wäsche pro Tag, sonntags acht Stunden bügeln. Wäschereibetrieb? Nein, das ist der ganz normale Alltag für Bettina Schneider
5 als Managerin einer Großfamilie. Die 40-jährige Mutter von acht Kindern lebt gemeinsam mit Papa Walter (52) und Hund Anton in *Zemmer*. Der Vorgarten lässt keinen Zweifel daran, dass hier alles auf
10 Kinder ausgelegt ist: Ein Schwimmbassin lädt zum Wasserspaß bei besserem Wetter ein, ein Holz-Häuschen schützt den Indoor-Sandkasten für die Kleinen, und auch die Schaukel fehlt nicht.

15 Vor dem Mittagessen muss Joshua, das älteste Kind, den Tisch decken. Er hat Küchendienst. Die Aufgabe teilt er sich reihum mit seinen Brüdern Alexander und Max. Heute gibt es Nudelauflauf
20 und Salat. Joshua muss auch Anna und Jonas, die dreijährigen Zwillinge, von der Haltestelle abholen, wo sie aus dem Kindergartenbus aussteigen. Im Haus landen Rucksäcke, Mützen und Schals
25 auf dem Boden. Bei acht Kindern ist der Geräuschpegel meistens sehr hoch. Das kann natürlich auch nerven, aber die Mutter sieht es positiv: „Es ist Leben im Haus. Ohne die Kinder würde mir etwas
30 fehlen."

Der kleine Elias hat eben auf Mamas Arm sein Milchfläschchen getrunken und liegt nun selig schlafend in seiner Babyschale. Die Zwillinge Jule und Emily
35 sorgen da für mehr Stimmung: Erst kippt Jule ihren Teller über dem Boden aus, dann fällt Emilys Teller mit den Nudeln hinunter. Macht nichts, denn Anton, der schwarze, drei Monate alte Hund, schleckt
40 alles auf.

Nach dem Essen kommt wieder Bewegung in die Familie: Joshua räumt die Spülmaschine ein und reicht seiner Mutter einen Kaffee. Dann bringt er Jonas wieder zum Bus, weil der Dreijährige 45 auch nachmittags in die Kita[1] möchte. Alexander fährt mit seinem Fußballverein nach *Trier* ins Kino.

Mutter Bettina zeigt Papa Walter einen ‚Gutschein', den Joshua ihr geschenkt 50 hat. Der ‚Gutschein' verspricht ein paar Stündchen auf der Couch, „die du sonst nie hast"—Joshua will für einen Tag die Hausarbeit übernehmen. Schließlich ist die einzige Auszeit, die Bettina genießt, der 55 dreistündige Großeinkauf ohne Kinder. Vater und Mutter bezweifeln, ob der gut gemeinte Vorschlag wirkliche Entlastung bedeutet. Walter ist ja schon länger dafür, eine Haushaltshilfe zu beschäftigen. „So 60 geht's nicht weiter", meint er. Das letzte Mal waren die Eltern vor zehn Jahren gemeinsam aus. Es gibt eben immer etwas zu tun.

Im Haus wollen sie in den kommenden 65 Wochen den Flur tapezieren und anstreichen und nächstes Jahr den Dachboden für die zwei ältesten Brüder umbauen. Dann könnten die vier Zwillinge aus dem elterlichen Schlafzimmer in das 70 frei werdende Kinderzimmer ziehen.

Plötzlich ist es wirklich ruhig im Haus. Emily und Jule schlafen in ihren Wippen in der Küche, Elias sowieso, Max führt mit einer seiner Freundinnen den Hund 75 spazieren und Joshua ist zu einem Freund gegangen.

Zwischen 17 und 19 Uhr ist es mit der Ruhe wieder vorbei. Es ist die lauteste

[1]die Kita: the day-care centre

80 Zeit des Tages. Die Kinder kehren zurück ins Haus. Um 18 Uhr gibt es Abendessen. Walter und Bettina machen die Kleinen vorher für die Nacht fertig. „Ohne Meckern und Maulen lassen sie sich ins
85 Bett bringen", freut sich Bettina. Aber bestimmte Rituale müssen sein: Mama muss noch ein paar Minuten Jules Hand halten. Das ist einer der Momente im Familientrubel, den auch die Mutter nicht
90 missen möchte. Papa muss Jonas und Anna noch zwei bis dreimal „Gute Nacht"

sagen. Elias schläft schon im Wohnzimmer. Max geht nochmal mit dem Hund raus. Dann machen sich auch die Ältesten gegen 20 Uhr fertig fürs Bett. Eine Stunde 95 dürfen Alexander und Max in ihrem Zimmer noch Musik hören oder lesen. Bei Joshua brennt noch bis halb zehn das Licht. Erst dann haben die Eltern Zeit für sich allein. Bis 6.30 Uhr ist jetzt 100 Ruhe. Dann beginnt ein neuer Tag bei Familie Schneider.

Marks

QUESTIONS

1. Read lines 1–14.

    (a) Why might the reader think that Bettina Schneider works in a laundry? 2

    (b) Apart from a swing, what else in the garden suggests that this family have children? Mention **two** things. 1

2. Read lines 15–48.

    (a) What **two** tasks does Joshua have before lunch today? 2

    (b) What happens to the plates of the two youngest twins, Jule and Emily? 2

    (c) Once lunch is over, what **exactly** does Joshua do? 2

3. Read lines 49–64.

    (a) Explain in detail the 'voucher' that Joshua has given his mother. 2

    (b) What is the mother's only respite in the week? 1

4. Read lines 65–71.

    (a) There are jobs to be done in the family house. What do the family plan to do:

        (i) in the next few weeks; 1

        (ii) next year? 1

    (b) What will happen when all this work is completed? 1

5. Read lines 72–77.

    Explain why it is suddenly peaceful in the house. Mention any **two** details. 2

6. Read lines 78–102.

    (a) What bedtime rituals take place each night:

        (i) for Jule; 1

        (ii) for Jonas and Anna? 1

    (b) When **exactly** do the parents get time to themselves each day? 1

    (20)

7. Translate into English:

    „Im Haus landen Rucksäcke . . . würde mir etwas fehlen." (lines 23–30) 10

    (30)

[Turn over for SECTION II on *Page four*

SECTION II—DIRECTED WRITING

Marks

Last Christmas you had the chance to go to one of the many Christmas markets which are held in Germany during the four weeks before Christmas. You stayed with the family of a German student you know.

When you return to Scotland, you write a report **in German** for the Languages department blog.

You must include the following information and **you should try to add** other relevant details:

- how you travelled to Germany **and** what you did during the journey
- where you stayed **and** how you got on with the whole family
- how you spent your time at the Christmas market
- what you thought of the different meals you ate
- what you did during the time you had to yourself during this visit
- what you would recommend about being in Germany just before Christmas **(15)**

Your report should be 150–180 words in length.

Marks will be deducted for any area of information that is omitted.

[END OF QUESTION PAPER]

X060/12/12

NATIONAL
QUALIFICATIONS
2013

FRIDAY, 24 MAY
3.00 PM – 4.00 PM

GERMAN
HIGHER
Listening Transcript

This paper must not be seen by any candidate.

The material overleaf is provided for use in an emergency only (eg the recording or equipment proving faulty) or where permission has been given in advance by SQA for the material to be read to candidates with additional support needs. The material must be read exactly as printed.

Instructions to reader(s):

The dialogue below should be read in approximately 4½ minutes. On completion of the first reading, pause for two minutes, then read the dialogue a second time.

Where special arrangements have been agreed in advance to allow the reading of the material, those sections marked **(m)** should be read by a male speaker and those marked **(f)** by a female.

Candidates have two minutes to study the questions before the transcript is read.

Karen, a German girl, who has been living and working abroad for five years, talks about her experiences.

(m) **Warum bist du nach Schottland gekommen?**

(f) Ich war mit der Realschule fertig und hatte auch keine Lust mehr auf Schule. Ich wollte ins Ausland gehen und als Au Pair arbeiten. Ja, und nach Schottland wollte ich auch schon immer mal. Also habe ich diese Ideen kombiniert und nach schottischen Au-Pair Agenturen gesucht, aber das war relativ schwierig. Schließlich habe ich eine Agentur gefunden, die mich dann vermittelt hat, und zwar nach Argyll in Westschottland.

(m) **Was war das für eine Familie?**

(f) Das war eine Familie mit zwei Kindern. Sie haben in einem großen Schloss gelebt, direkt am Meer, das war also sehr schön. Es war nicht so schön, dass ich die ganze Hausarbeit machen sollte.

(m) **War das zuviel Arbeit?**

(f) Ja, aber die ganze Situation war noch viel schlimmer, denn die Eltern hatten mir nicht gesagt, dass sie das Schloss manchmal als Hotel vermieten. Ungefähr zweimal im Monat musste ich mit den Kindern ausziehen, weil Gäste kamen, die das Schloss für ein Wochenende oder eine Woche gemietet hatten.

(m) **Wie lange warst du denn bei dieser Familie?**

(f) Ich glaube, ich bin im September hingefahren aber bin nach zwei Monaten oder so wieder gegangen. Ich habe den Eltern gesagt, dass mir die Situation nicht gefällt und ich so nicht arbeiten wollte. Und dann hat mich die Agentur nach Fochabers vermittelt, zu einer Familie mit drei Kindern.

(m) **Wie lange warst du dann bei dieser Familie?**

(f) Von Mitte November bis April im nächsten Jahr.

(m) **Und was hast du bei dieser Familie machen müssen?**

(f) Also die Situation bei dieser Familie war komplett anders. Die Familie hat auf einem Bauernhof gelebt und hatte drei Kinder im Alter von drei, fünf und sieben Jahren. Ich war hauptsächlich für die Kinder da und nicht für den Haushalt verantwortlich.

(m) **War das nach deinem Geschmack?**

(f) Ja, das war gut. Wir haben praktisch jede freie Minute draußen verbracht. Wir haben uns um die Tiere gekümmert und Dinge gemacht, die nichts mit Fernsehen oder Rumsitzen zu tun hatten. Wenn das Wetter ganz schlecht war, haben wir Modelle gebaut oder etwas Anderes im Haus gemacht.

(m) **Und was hast du anschließend gemacht?**

(f) Anfang April bin ich nach Kanada geflogen und habe den ganzen Sommer auf der Beaver Lodge gearbeitet. Ich habe dort kleine Gruppen von Touristen auf Pferden durch die Rocky Mountains geführt.

(m)   **Bist du danach wieder nach Deutschland gegangen?**

(f)   Nein, dann bin ich nach Schottland zurückgekommen. Innerhalb einer Woche habe ich eine Wohnung gefunden und mit meinem ersten Jahr am College angefangen, um meine Highers in Englisch, Physik und Chemie zu machen.

(m)   **Und was machst du jetzt?**

(f)   Mittlerweile studiere ich Umweltwissenschaften und bin jetzt im zweiten Jahr von meinem Bachelor-Studium.

(m)   **OK, und wie gefällt es dir?**

(f)   Es ist wirklich gut. Ich habe jetzt endlich das gefunden, was mich echt interessiert. Es geht definitiv in die Richtung, in der ich später arbeiten möchte.

(m)   **Und zwar?**

(f)   Wenn ich fertig bin, hoffe ich in einem Naturpark oder einem Wildlife Centre zu arbeiten, so etwas in der Richtung. Als ich in Kanada war, habe ich schon ein Jobangebot bekommen. Mehrere Leute haben mir gesagt, ich soll mich bei ihnen melden, wenn ich ein Praktikum oder einen Job suche.

[END OF TRANSCRIPT]

[BLANK PAGE]

FOR OFFICIAL USE

Examiner's Marks	
A	
B	

Total Mark

X060/12/02

NATIONAL
QUALIFICATIONS
2013

FRIDAY, 24 MAY
3.00 PM – 4.00 PM

GERMAN
HIGHER
Listening/Writing

Fill in these boxes and read what is printed below.

Full name of centre

Town

Forename(s)

Surname

Date of birth

Day   Month   Year   Scottish candidate number   Number of seat

Do not open this paper until told to do so.

Answer Section A **in English** and Section B **in German**.

Section A

Listen carefully to the recording with a view to answering, **in English**, the questions printed in this answer book. Write your answers **clearly and legibly** in the spaces provided after each question.

You will have 2 minutes to study the questions before hearing the dialogue for the first time.

The dialogue will be played **twice**, with an interval of 2 minutes between the two playings.

You may make notes at any time but only in this answer book. **Score out any notes before you hand in the book.**

Move on to Section B when you have completed Section A: you will **not** be told when to do this.

Section B

Do not write your response in this book: **use the 4 page lined answer sheet**.

You will be told to insert the answer sheet inside this book before handing in your work.

You may consult a German dictionary at any time during **both** sections.

Before leaving the examination room you must give this book to the Invigilator. If you do not, you may lose all the marks for this paper.

Section A

Marks

Karen, a German girl, who has been living and working abroad for five years, talks about her experiences.

1. Why did Karen come to Scotland? Mention **two** things.

   2

2. (*a*) What does she tell you about the first family she worked for? Mention **two** things.

   2

   (*b*) What was not so nice?

   1

3. (*a*) What had the parents not told her?

   1

   (*b*) What did Karen have to do because of this?

   1

4. (*a*) How long did Karen spend with this family?

   1

   (*b*) What did she say to the parents? Mention any **one** thing.

   1

5. What sort of accommodation did the second family have?

   1

Marks

6. (*a*) What did Karen particularly like about her work with this family?   **1**

   (*b*) How did she and the children spend their time together? Mention any **two** things.   **2**

7. What did she do in her summer job at Beaver Lodge in Canada?   **1**

8. What did she do, when she came back to Scotland? Mention **two** things.   **2**

9. What is she doing now?   **1**

10. Why is she enjoying this?   **1**

11. In what way might her experience in Canada help her in the future? Mention **two** things.   **2**

(20)

[Turn over for Section B on *Page four*

Section B

Karen hat nach der Schule Verschiedenes gemacht.   Was willst du in der Zukunft machen? Möchtest du auch woanders leben?

Schreibe 120 – 150 Worte zu diesen Fragen!

10

(30)

USE THE 4 PAGE LINED ANSWER SHEET FOR YOUR ANSWER TO SECTION B

[END OF QUESTION PAPER]

[BLANK PAGE]

Acknowledgements

Permission has been sought from all relevant copyright holders and Hodder Gibson is grateful for the use of the following:

The article 'Von Limo zu Sex on the Beach' by Florian Thalmann taken from the newspaper 'Sachsische Zeiturg', Jurge Szene, 16th August 2007 © Sachsische Zeitung GmbH (2009 Reading & Directed Writing pages 2–3);

The article 'Neue Heimat' by Andrea Walter taken from 'Brigitte Young Miss', November 2005 © G+J Women New Media GmbH (2010 Reading & Directed Writing pages 2–3);

The article 'Hinter den Kulissen des Tourismus' taken from Kölner Stadt-Anzeiger, 23 July 2009 © Mediengruppe M. Dumont Schauberg GmbH & Co. KG (2011 Reading & Directed Writing pages 2–3);

The article Wenn einer eine Reise tut...' taken from the newspaper Kölner Stadt-Anzeiger, 21 July 2010 © Mediengruppe M. Dumont Schauberg GmbH & Co. KG (2012 Reading & Directed Writing pages 2–3);

The article 'Familie Schneider hat acht Kinder—Ein Tag mit einer Großfamilie' by Sybille Schonhofen, adapted from 'Trierishcher Volksfreund, 5/6 April 2008. Section: Wochenendjournal © Volksfreund-Druckerei Nikolaus Koch GmbH (2013 Reading & Directed Writing pages 2–3).

HIGHER | ANSWER SECTION

SECTION I – READING

1. (a) *Any one of:*
   - what people/they enjoy about/in the summer (time)
   - people/they love/enjoy/everyone loves the sun, warmth/warm weather/heat and free time in the summer
   - sun, warmth and free time are the best things/their favourite things about summer

   (b) • how people use/spend free/leisure/spare time
     how one uses one's free time
     the use of free time
     what they do/did in their free time

2. (a) • they <u>had to</u>/<u>would</u>/<u>used to</u> walk/run, as there were no buses

   (b) • met/collected/picked up/fetched/got tourists from the ferry
     went to tourists at the ferry
     • took/carried/brought/dropped off/put their (suit)cases/luggage/bags to guest houses/B&B/inn/hotel/place they were staying brought their cases to the guest house

   (c) *Any two from:*
     • worked in a milk(-shake) bar/milk-shake shop
     • went walking/hiking <u>a lot</u>/on <u>a lot of</u>/<u>many</u> walks <u>lots of</u> walking tours
     • <u>sometimes</u> went to the Baltic (on holiday).

3. • They took/brought food with them/they took their own food/they had their own food/lunch.
   • If/when they had the money, they bought/would buy <u>a bottle of</u> lemonade/(fizzy-)juice.

4. (a) *Any one of:*
     • They made/sewed/stitched/cut/tailored their own clothes/things.
       Clothes that they altered themselves.
     • Dresses and skirts/a dress and skirt
     • They rolled/bunched/pulled up/folded over/adjusted their skirts to turn them into mini-skirts.
       They wore skirts high as mini-skirts.

   (b) • (They wore) mini-skirts and shorts.
     OR
     • The summer colour was blue.

   (c) *Any one of:*
     • lots of/many colours are fashionable/topical/up-to-date/in fashion/in.
       the current trend is to wear lots of colours.
     • people often wear stripes/stripes are popular/worn a lot/often.
     • lots of colours and stripes.

5. (a) • The only parties were family ones/celebrations.
       Parties were a family thing.
       Parties would be for families.
       There were only family parties.
       They were only at family festivals.
     • The children/young people/you <u>had to</u> be home/in/in the house at/by midnight.
       You <u>had to</u> go back to the house/home by/for midnight.

   (b) • they go to the disco/clubbing/night-clubs <u>every weekend</u>/<u>most weekends</u>/<u>every week</u>/<u>at the weekends</u>.
     • go to/visit town/city festivals/parties/celebrations/fairs/fêtes/galas/fiestas.

6. • Oma Ingrid – sang hiking/hiker/rambling/walking songs/ they sang songs while they were walking/hiking.
   • Katrin Bredner – they recorded/taped their own voices/music/tunes (on a cassette recorder) <u>and</u> listened to it.

7. • The sun was very/really important <u>to/for her</u>. She found the sun very important.
   • She/you/one <u>could</u>/<u>was able to</u>/<u>got to</u> relax/take it easy/unwind.

8. Wir sind aber nie in den Urlaub gefahren
   But/However/we never/did not ever go/went (away/anywhere)/would never go (away/anywhere)/never used to go (away/anywhere)/on holiday/vacation/for a holiday

   weil wir nicht genug Geld hatten
   because/as/since/we did not have/didn't have/hadn't enough money.

   Meine Mutter sagte oft zu uns Kinder:
   My mother/mum often said/used to say/would say to us children/kids

   „Ich möchte so gerne einmal mit euch in die Bergen fahren…"
   I would/I'd so/really like/I would/I'd so love to go/to travel/to drive/to the mountains with you/one day/some day/sometime/(just) once/.

   Sie wollte uns immer die Alpen zeigen.
   She always wanted/was wanting to show us the Alps.

SECTION II – DIRECTED WRITING

Please see the table on pages 93–94 which provides details of the criteria required to produce a good essay answer.

HIGHER GERMAN LISTENING/WRITING 2009

SECTION A

1. 4,500

2. (a) • relatively few(er)/only a few/very few/not many/not a lot/too little/very little/hardly any/not very many/not enough for the number of people
   fewer/less places than the number of students.

   (b) *Any one from:*
   • to leave/move out of Görlitz/their town/home/parents/ friends.
   • to go to/find/get a place/one in another town/city/ place.
   • to move away/to another town.

3. *Any two from:*
   • not (so) easy.
   • <u>missed</u> her friends/family/home area.
   • knew nobody/did not know anyone.

4. • can bring/take friends home at any time/no matter how late it is/until as late as she wants/when(ever) she wants/at any time of the day/regardless of the time/as late as she likes.
   • <u>at weekend</u> can sleep (in)/lie in/stay in bed as late/long as you want/long lies.
   can get up whenever he wants.
   sleep all weekend.

5. *Any three from:*
   • You have to/must/having to do everything (for) yourself
   She has to/must/having to do everything (for) herself.
   • (You have/she has to do) your/her own shopping/the shopping/buy things for herself/buy everything/shop for herself/pay for her own shopping.
   • (You have) to clean yourself/(she has) to clean herself/do your/her own cleaning/the cleaning/the housework/clean the house.
   • (You have/she has) to budget/make sure money lasts to the end of the month/work out the finances/divide up the money (for the month)/manage your money/keep track of your money/organise your finances for each month.

6. • She is earning/making/earns/gets/makes more money (than friends in Görlitz).
   She has been able to earn more money than her friends.
   She is better paid in Hamburg.
   (You get/earn/make) more money.
   Her old friends in Görlitz earn less than her.

7. (a) • A colleague/employee/trainee/someone took/was ill.

   (b) • She wanted to live/stay in North(ern) Germany.

8. • They went/travelled/came with her to Hamburg.
   They went to Hamburg together.
   They took her to Hamburg.
   • They looked/searched together/with her for a flat/house/ somewhere to stay/a place to stay/live/accommodation.
   They helped her look for/find/get/visit a flat.
   They viewed flats with her.
   They found a flat with her.
   • They bought her/paid for everything/things/stuff/items/what she needed/everything she needed <u>for the flat/house.</u>
   They helped her buy everything <u>for the flat.</u>

9. • Hamburg is (very/so) <u>much/a lot/lots</u> bigger/larger.
   One is a big city; the other is a town.
   • The people speak/have/talk a different/their own dialect.
   The dialect is different/there are different dialects.
   The people speak a different kind of German.

10. *Any one from:*
    • To see/meet (up with)/visit/catch up with her <u>old/childhood</u> friends.
    To see the friends she had there.
    To see her friends again.

11. • She is <u>more</u> independent/grown-up/self-sufficient/self-reliant/mature.
    She is more of an adult.
    She has gained in independence.
    She can <u>now</u> stand on her own two feet.

SECTION B

Please see the table on pages 96–97 which provides details of the criteria required to produce a good essay answer.

HIGHER GERMAN
READING AND DIRECTED WRITING
2010

SECTION I – READING

1. *Any one from:*
   - To go/be/live somewhere where nobody would know her/where nobody knew/knows her/who she was
     Because everyone knew her as the minister's daughter
   - As the minister's/priest's/pastor's/vicar's/reverend's daughter you cannot get drunk/let yourself get drunk
   - As the minister's/priest's/pastor's/vicar's daughter you do not want to embarrass your parents

2. (a) • People who (would) tell her/explain to her/describe to her what it is like/how it is somewhere else/elsewhere
       • People who tell her what other places are like/what it is like in other places/how other places are/were
         People who tell her how it is living elsewhere

   (b) *Any two from:*
       • They vetoed it/they told her she could not go
         They wanted to put a stop to the idea
         They put a veto on it/her
         They tried to veto it/they said she was not allowed
         They put a veto on South Africa
         They exercised their veto/they put a veto in place
         They laid down their veto
         They prohibited her
         They forbad her
         They tried to stop her
       • They were/are worried
         They worried (about it/the idea)
         They worried about her
         They got themselves worried
         It worried them
         They had their worries
       • (They said) the streets are not safe for a woman/girl
         a woman/girl/lady cannot/should not go out in the street
         You cannot go on/into/wander/walk (down) the street(s) as a woman
         It is not a place for women to be alone on the street

3. • (She told them that) they had brought her up/taught her to be independent
     they had taught her independence/to think for herself
     they had made her independent
     they gave her independence
   • Now they were trying/wanting to take an important decision away from her/out of her hands
     Parents wanted to take the decision into their own hands
     They were now trying/wanting to take away her independence
     It was not right that they were trying to take away her independence
     She said did they want to take this important decision out of her hands?

4. • That is her leaving the house/home for ever
     That is her gone for good from home/the house
     She is going to be out of the house for ever
     That's her out of the house for ever
     She has left home for good
     She won't come to live at home again
   • When she comes back, she won't be my little girl anymore
     She will never come back/return as his/my little daughter
     My little girl isn't coming back
     He will never get his little daughter back

She comes back no more/longer as his little daughter
She can no longer go back to being his little girl
She won't come back as his little girl

5. *Any four from:*
   (a) • Makes/gets/prepares/cooks breakfast
         Made/got/prepared/cooked breakfast
       • Takes/brings children to school
         Took/brought children to school
       • Goes to fitness studio/gym
         Went to fitness studio/gym
       • Lies in sun/sunbathes/sits in sun
         Lay in sun/sunbathed/sat in sun
       • Reads (a lot)
         Any four for 2 marks; 2 or 3 for 1 mark; less than 2 = 0 marks

   (b) • Make/get/give the children/kids a snack/something to eat
       • Play with the children until the parents come (home/back)/get home/are home/return/arrive

6. (a) • Host/Guest father asked his colleague/Karel to take Annette to clubs/to go to clubs with Annette/to go clubbing with Annette
         He was a colleague of the father and the father asked him to take Annette to clubs
       • So that she would see young (life in) Cape Town/young people's Cape Town
         So that she would see/meet the youth of/young people in Cape Town
         So that she would not be bored

   (b) • She wanted/would like to stay there, study there, live/stay/have a life with Karel

7. • To look at/see how she was living/what her lifestyle is
     To see what her life was like
   • (To see) who this guy was who was messing everything up/upsetting everything/the cause of all the confusion/who brought all the confusion/who brought about this muddle/who brought this mess together/who made everything confusing

8. • To apply to study/go to university/college in Cape Town
     To apply for a study/student place in Cape Town
     To apply for her studies in Cape Town

9. • Time will tell where they will end up
     They are leaving (it) open whether to stay in South Africa/go back to Germany
     They do not know whether they will stay in Cape Town/go back to Germany
     They do not know whether they will leave Cape Town/stay in Germany
     They will see whether or not they will leave Cape Town/stay in Germany
   • They have no plans other than/but to enjoy life (now)
     Their only plan is to enjoy life
     No more plans – (to) enjoy life

10. Karel kommt über Weihnachten und Silvester nach Deutschland.
    Karel came/comes to Germany over/for Christmas and New Year/New Year's Eve/Hogmanay/New Years

    Als es Zeit für den Rückflug ist,
    When it was/is time for the flight back/for the return flight/to fly back

    freut sich Annette und ist zugleich sehr traurig.
    Annette was/is happy/glad/pleased/delighted and (yet) (is/was) very sad at the same time/Annette is both happy and very sad at the same time

,,Ich weiß, dass es für meine Familie schwer ist,
I know that it/this is/it's/hard/difficult/tough for/on my family

aber es ist bestimmt die richtige Entscheidung für mich.
but/however it/this is definitely/certainly the right/correct decision for me.

SECTION II – DIRECTED WRITING

Please see the table on pages 93–94 which provides details of the criteria required to produce a good essay answer.

SECTION A

1. (*a*) • July 2009/last July/<u>almost/nearly</u> a year ago
      Almost a year ago in July

   (*b*) • 6 weeks

2. • (part-time) job/she has a job/she got a job/she has a wee job
      Savings/she has saved some money
   • Parents (pay the rest)

3. • Had a visit from a cousin from the US
      Cousin from America visited them
      Had a cousin over from the States
      American cousin visited them
   • Told her (a lot) about it/US/the States/America
      Explained/talked about it/US etc.
      Told stories about it/US etc
      Cousin was always talking about it/US etc

4. *Any two from:*
   • You hear so much about it/them
   • Is it like it is in films?/Are they like they are in films?
      She wants to see (for herself) if they are like they are in films
      If the films portray them accurately
      Are the movies accurate?
      She wants to know if everything is really like it looks in the films
   • Is it/school more fun than at home/in Germany?
      School looks more fun than in Germany
      American schools look like fun
      American schools look/seem more fun
      She wants to know if schools are more fun in America
      She feels she will have more fun in school there
      She thinks school in America is more fun than in Germany.
      Wants to see how fun it is compared with her school

5. *Any two from:*
   • Landscape/countryside/scenery
   • Cultural differences
      The differences between the cultures
      The different culture/The culture is different
      Learning about different culture(s)
   • Its/the country's variety
      The (many) different aspects/sides of the country
      The many (different) sides of the country

6. • One hour in <u>car</u>/an hour's <u>drive</u> from Chicago

7. • 11 months
      From August to July

8. (*a*) • Pleased/happy/glad/delighted/joyful for her
         Happy she is getting such an opportunity
      • It will be hard/difficult (for her)
         She will find it hard when Rica is away
         She will find it hard when she goes
         She will find it hard to cope
         She thinks it will be hard.

   (*b*) • Good/great that she has this possibility/ opportunity/ chance/ option
         It's a good/great opportunity (for her)
         They are happy that she has this opportunity
         It's good to have the opportunity

9. • Things to remember best friend by
      Things to remind her of best friend
      Keepsake(s)/Memory pieces from her best friend
      Reminders of her best friend

Precious gift from her best friend
Presents/Personal objects from her best friend(s)
- Piano (sheet) music/notes/books/pieces
- German recipes/Granny's recipes

10. • Quite a distance (away)
(Quite/too/very/rather/really) far (away)
A long way/journey/distance (away)

11. *Any one from:*
- <u>More</u> self-confidence/to be more self-confident
<u>More</u> confident in herself
<u>More</u> self-assured
- <u>More</u> independence/to be more independent
<u>More</u> self-sufficient

SECTION B

Please see the table on pages 96–97 which provides details of the criteria required to produce a good essay answer.

HIGHER GERMAN READING AND DIRECTED WRITING 2011

SECTION I – READING

1. *Any three from:*
   - Holiday-makers/they sun themselves/bask/sit in the sun/sunbathe/catch/worship the sun/get a tan at/on the square/ in front of/at/outside the/a café
   Must have sun <u>and</u> venue
   - Families coming back from/straight in off the beach/shore
   - (Families/They) have/do not begrudge themselves a cool/cold drink
   - Children have/eat an ice-cream/ice-lolly

2. (a) • People who work/help <u>in the big hotel(s)</u>
   Helpers/Assistants/Workers/Employees/Staff <u>in/from/of (the) big hotel(s)</u>

   (b) • Island 17 kilometres long and a few/not many hundred metres wide
   • Not much work/They don't get a lot of work
   <u>Hotel owner(s)</u> live(s) off summer income
   • Children have to go to mainland/leave the island for (secondary/grammar/higher) school(ing)/education
   • In medical emergencies/For medical assistance reliant/you have to rely on/fly by/be airlifted by helicopter
   The medical problems rely on emergency helicopters
   Medical provision in an emergency depends on a helicopter
   Medical supplies/provisions provided/brought by helicopter in an emergency
   Emergencies have to be taken by helicopter

3. • long white sand(y) beach(es)/shores
   long stretch/strips of white sand
   walk along/absorb long white sandy beaches
   • (good) sea(side)/ocean air/breeze free of/without/away from car/exhaust fumes/emissions/gas(es) from cars/car pollution/car exhaust/car fumes
   The smell of the sea without the smell of car exhaust fumes
   Take in the good sea air instead of car fumes
   Clean sea air because it is not polluted by cars
   Good smell of the sea and not car exhaust fumes

4. (a) • She was the only temp/seasonal/part-time worker in the café
   She was the only helper/assistant in the café

   (b) *Any one from:*
   • Someone else <u>the same age</u> came/another person h<u>er age/of similar age</u> came/followed/ joined
   Another girl <u>her age</u> joined the café to help out
   She got to know/found/met/got a colleague <u>of the same age</u>.
   • She learned/found out that a lot of young people/teenagers/youths from elsewhere/outside the island/out-of-town worked on the island/there
   She learned that a lot of foreign young people worked on the island

   (c) • The locals/residents/islanders/natives went to the same bars/pubs as the holiday-makers/people on holiday
   Inhabitants, visitors and temporary workers all met there/You can meet everyone there/The variety of people that went there all the time

5. (a) • Cups/Mugs and glasses fell off her tray/A cup/mug and glass fell off her tray
She dropped/broke cups/mugs and glasses off her tray.

(b) • She wanted to cash up at one table but did not look at the bill
She tried to charge the wrong customer for 11 beers/She charged someone for beer they did not drink
She gave the wrong bill (to a/the customer)
She mixed up table numbers when giving the bill

6. • They were not sympathetic/did not show any understanding/had little understanding/sense/did not understand/did not care about when/that the café wanted to close/it was closing time/they were about to close/they were about to shut the café
• They do not understand…
…that the staff want/long to go home after working a 12 hour shift
…that the staff couldn't wait to stop work after 12 hours
…that the staff want to see/yearn for an end to their 12 hour working day
…that they had had enough after working 12 hours
…that the staff work 12 hour shifts and that it is their time to stop work

7. (a) • She can guess/predict what they are going to order/She knows their order before they say it/ She gets to know what they order/She can, after they have been back several times, order for them/You know what they order/She remembers their orders
• the nice/friendly/good conversations/chat(s)/talk/discussion (with them)

(b) • The ones who cannot/will not/would not/do not want to wait 10 minutes for a coffee/to be served

8. Für uns bedeutet das: Hektik.
For/To us/ourselves
that/this/it means/signifies/represents
meant/signified/represented
it/that means/meant this:

For us that means one thing:
That is what it means for us:

(a) hectic pace/atmosphere.
(a) hectic rush(es).
a hectic time/hectic times
(a) mad rush.
hustle and bustle

For us that means (that) it is (going to be) hectic.

That means a mad rush for us.

Bestellungen aufnehmen und servieren,
Taking (down/in) orders
Record(ing)

and serving them/orders
Taking and serving orders
Orders to take and serve
To take and serve orders
Orders (have) to be taken and served.
Orders are taken and served.
Take a note of orders and serve them.
Take/taking (a note of) orders and serve/serving
We have to take and serve orders

nebenbei den Spülberg in Zaum halten
(whilst) at the same time
at the same time as
(and) in addition/additionally

besides/alongside/along with
as well as/incidentally
while/whilst (also)

(having) to keep/keeping

in check/under control
a check on/check of/control of
on top of/up with
up to date with/a tight rein on

staying in control of/on top of/up to date with

the pile(s)/mountain(s)/heaps of dishes
the pile/mountain of washing-up
the pile of dish-washing

needs to be kept in check

und zwischendurch Geschenke aus dem Souvenirladen einpacken
and

in between times/this/that
between times/that/this
occasionally
in between
between all of that
meanwhile/in the meantime

wrap/wrapping (up)
pack/packing (up)
package/packaging
having to wrap/pack(age)
we/I have to wrap/pack(age)
the wrapping of

presents/gifts

from/out of the souvenir shop
the souvenir shop gifts

– nach solchen Tagen bin ich abends todmüde ins Bett gefallen.
after/on days/a day like this/that
after/on such days/such a day
after these/those days
after these kinds of days/this kind of day

I fell into (my) bed
I would fall into bed
I dropped into bed

in the evening(s)
at night
by the evening
of an evening

dead beat
dead(ly) tired
totally tired
so/very tired
(completely) exhausted
(totally/absolutely) shattered

SECTION II – DIRECTED WRITING

Please see the table on pages 93–94 which provides details of the criteria required to produce a good essay answer.

HIGHER GERMAN LISTENING/WRITING 2011

SECTION A

1. (a) • (little) village in north-east

   (b) *Any threee from:*
   - Very/Really nice
   - (Parents and she) had a good feeling/felt good about the family/Good feeling between the families/ Parents were happy to let her stay with them
   - Feels good/happy/is comfortable with the family/She gets on well with them/She feels at home with the family/They make her feel comfortable/She has a good relationship with them/The family is/are hospitable
   - Daughter is in the same class(es)/year

2. *Any two from:*
   - A friend was there two years ago
   - Class/year 11 pupils go abroad/to foreign/different/other countries
   - Can speak English fluently/Wants to speak English fluently/ Wants to improve her English/So she could learn better English/So she can practise her English/So that she can make her English flow

3. *Any one from:*
   - Does not <u>have/need</u> to share with brothers/sisters/ siblings/anyone/Does not <u>have/need</u> to share things/ anything
   - Gets/enjoys full attention of parents/Gets/Has parents all to herself/Parents' attention is never divided

4. *Any one from:*
   - The house is quiet/peaceful/She is a quiet/peaceful person and likes a quiet house/She enjoys the peace when she is home alone/It is quieter in the house which is good Quiet person — quiet house/A quiet household suits her
   - She is used to spending time alone

5. • You/They <u>have to/must/need</u> to share/One/She has to share (a room/at dinner-time)
   - Competition for food/when eating food/Mealtimes are a competition
   - Everyone takes 3 pieces of pizza at the start/at once/You have to take 3 pieces of pizza quickly

6. • Discuss/Agree/Talk about/(Pre-)Arrange when you/each person can use it/have the bathroom/toilet/have a bath Discuss who will use the bathroom first/Everyone has to decide when they will use the bathroom/Arrange who goes first
   - There are several/more/many/multiple bathrooms/There is more than 1 bathroom

7. *Any three from:*
   - They have lots of friends who drop in/visit/come over/come round The house is full of people as they have lots of friends They have lots of friends so the house is always busy
   - (Go to) visit friends
   - Spend <u>evenings/nights</u> singing/doing karaoke/having fun
   - Go to Inverness shopping (often)

8. *Any two from:*
   - They are so/very nice/kind/friendly/How nice they are
   - Not difficult to get on/along with people Gets along well with people/Finds it easy to get on with people
   - (Not difficult) to talk to strangers/people in supermarket (queue) If you are in the queue, they are friendly to you In the supermarket they talk to strangers

9. *Any two from:*
   - Happy/Glad/Good/Pleased/Excited/Can't wait to see her friends/She will enjoy seeing her friends/Looking forward to seeing her friends/Glad to be back with her family and friends
   - Will miss life in Scotland/the people/her Scottish family/ her friends here
   - It will be strange/funny not to see the people here every day

SECTION B

Please see the table on pages 96–97 which provides details of the criteria required to produce a good essay answer.

HIGHER GERMAN
READING AND DIRECTED WRITING
2012

SECTION I – READING

1. (a) • Via/through/over/on the Internet
On the Internet page of *Couchsurfing*
Via the Couchsurfing website
They were looking for somewhere to stay in
Washington DC and met them on the Internet.

   (b) *Any one from:*
   • They are the same age as the writer/Anja.
   They are in the same age-group/range as Anja.
   They are a similar age to Anja.
   They are the same age as us.

   • They gave Anja (and her boyfriend) a couch to sleep on
   Their couch was available
   They have a couch at their disposal
   They have their couches to offer
   Anja and boyfriend stayed/slept on their couch

2. *Any four from:*
   • They dry (more) quickly/fast(er)/are (more) quick drying/quick to dry.
   • They absorb/soak up (more) water/
   They are (more) (water)- absorbent/They suck up (more) water.
   • (Everything/It is/They are) (more) practical/handy
   • It washes (more) quickly/(more) quickly washable/can be washed (more) quickly/quick(er) to wash/ /they wash fast(er).
   • It is light(er)/(more) lightweight/light(er) material
   It makes their luggage lighter.
   Any 4 for two marks; 2 or 3 for one mark.

3. (a) • **Before they left** they gave up/resigned from/quit/left their (secure) jobs/gave/handed in their notice.

   (b) • To be influenced by nothing/nobody.
   No person/thing should/to influence them.
   To be under nobody's influence/With nobody to influence them/Nobody will be able to influence them.
   To stop being influenced by anyone.
   So that nobody could influence what they were doing.
   Without any outside pressure or influence.

   • Simply/Just (want) to live for two years
   To live this way for 2 years
   Simply 2 years of living
   This was 2 years simply to <u>live</u>/<u>just</u> to live.
   They are going to live their own way for 2 years.
   Simply to have 2 years to themselves

4. (a) • They sold their flat/apartment/house/accommodation **and** car.

   • They stored the (most) important/valuable things/stuff with their parents/at their parents'.
   They gave the (most) important things to their parents to store/to look after.
   They left/kept the (most) important things with their parents/at their parents'.

   • They gave the rest/everything else/the remainder away/to other people.
   They gifted the rest to other people.

   (b) • (On the one hand) sad to be leaving **friends and family**
   Sad - she would miss her **friends and family**

   • (On the other hand) pleased/delighted/thrilled/

excited/happy/joyful/glad/looking forward to be going on a world trip/tour/to be going round the world/to see the world

5. • Coming to terms/Coping/Having to deal with/Getting over disappointment(s)/being disappointed/To be rid of feelings of disappointment

   • (Especially/Particularly) if/when something is not as/what/how they/you expected/imagined
   If something is not like the expectations you had
   If something does/did not live up to expectations
   If something is different from the expectations/what they thought it was going to be

6. • It was cheaper to fly/go home first and then fly to South Africa than to fly from South America to South Africa.
   Cheaper to fly to South Africa from their home country/home than from South America to South Africa.
   More expensive to fly direct from South America to South Africa than to fly home first then to South Africa.

7. *Any two from:*
   • They do not/Danny does not have a clue.
   They have no idea.
   They have/Jillian has no **fixed/firm/solid/definite** plan(s).

   • Study **or** return to their careers/occupation/resume her/their occupation/start their career again/return to their job
   Study **or** continue with their career/work/Go in to their profession again

   • They don't (even) know what town or state they will/want/are going to live in.
   They are not sure what town or state they will live in.
   They need to decide what town or state they will live in.

8. (a) • Relationship/It is (a lot) closer/tighter/They have a (much) tighter relationship/They are (a lot) closer/ They have become (a lot/much) closer…
   … as/because they are together all the time/the whole time/because of all the time they spent together/because they were together all the time.

   (b) • They/You cannot run/get away/escape/flee from each other's moods/if one (of them/you) is in a mood/the other person's moods

   They/You have to learn how to cope/deal with/work through/handle each other's moods.
   You have to learn how to cope when one is in a mood.
   You have to face them and learn how to deal with them.

   • They cannot hide (their) feeling(s).
   You cannot hide (your) feeling(s).

9. „Ich vermisse den Lebensstil, den wir aufgegeben haben,
   "I miss

   the lifestyle
   the style/way of life

   that/which
   omission of "that/which"

   we have given up
   we gave up

   den Fitnessclub, eine gesunde Ernährung, Wochenendausflüge.
   the fitness club/centre/studio
   the leisure club/centre/studio
   the gym

   a healthy diet
   eating healthy/healthily
   healthy eating/nutrition
   healthy nourishment

(eating) healthy food
a healthy way of eating
healthy eating habits

Ignore addition of 'and'

weekend trips.
weekend outings.
weekend excursions.
outings/trips/excursions at the weekend.

Aber ich möchte jetzt keinen Job, in dem ich von 9 bis 17 Uhr
arbeite
But/However

I wouldn't/would not like (to have) a/any job
I would not want a/any job
I would like no job

now

in which
where

I am working
I work
I worked/were working

(from) 9 (am) to 5 (pm)
(from) 9 (am) till/until 5 (pm)
From 9 to 5 o'clock

*But I would like to have no job now where I am working from 9
to 5.*

und Papier auf dem Schreibtisch herumschiebe", meint Danny.
and

push
move
shove
(pushing/moving/shoving – following on from earlier sections)

paper/papers

around the/my (writing) desk,"
round on the/my desk,"

push around paper(s) on the/my desk,"

says/states/thinks/opines Danny.
said/stated/thought/opined Danny.

Auch Jillian vermisst die alltäglichen Dinge, die ihr früher auf
die Nerven gingen.
Jillian too/also
Also Jillian

misses

the everyday things
the day-to-day things
the ordinary/routine things

which/that

got/have got on her nerves
annoyed/have annoyed her
irritated/have irritated her
got her annoyed

before/previously/formerly
in the past/earlier

which used to get on her nerves.
which had previously annoyed her.
which once got on her nerves.

SECTION II – DIRECTED WRITING

Please see the table on pages 93–94 which provides details of the
criteria required to produce a good essay answer.

HIGHER GERMAN LISTENING/WRITING 2012

SECTION A

1. (a) • It is (quite) typical/normal/It exists.
   It is common./It belongs to daily life.

   (b) • Australia **and** New Zealand

2. *Any two from:*
   • Knee-length skirt
   • Dark/navy-blue (skirt)
   • White blouse/shirt

3. • You all/always have the **same** things on/wear the **same** things.
   Everyone wears the **same** things/had the **same** clothes.
   Everyone is/looks/dresses the **same**.
   Everyone was/dressed/looked the **same**.
   It was the **same** clothes every day.

   • You don't need to think about/choose/decide/worry about/organise/plan/pick out what to put on/wear.

4. • They made/make their skirt(s) short(er)/shortened their skirts/rolled up their skirt(s).

   • They decorated their blazer(s) with badges/pins.
   They put/stick/wore badges/pins on their blazers/pins.
   Blazers with badges/pins

5. *Any one from:*
   • (They had) extreme/punk hair-styles/haircuts
   Exaggerated hair-style/Extreme haircuts/hair colours

   • (They wore) big/large/huge ear-rings

6. • She changed into them/her fashion gear/fashionable clothes as soon as/when she got home.
   She (always) wears them at home.
   After school she changes into them.
   Only when she got home from school.
   She wears them when not in school.
   When she came home she had to be in her designer clothes.

7. • They did/do not have the/enough money for them.
   They cost too much./They are too dear.
   They cannot afford them.
   They are/were not cheap.
   (They are) expensive.
   The cost

8. • Hand-me-downs – Any response which shows an understanding of getting clothes worn by another member of the family e.g.
   Some pupils have to wear a uniform they got from their sister or cousin.

   • They/The poorer ones only have/can only afford two (white) blouses/shirts.
   People with rich parents have more blouses/shirts.
   The poorer ones cannot change as often.

9. • They have 4 or 5 blouses/shirts/tops
   They have 4/5 blouses/shirts

   • Which mother irons **every day**
   Which mother **always** ironed
   Which are **always** ironed

10. • Had to report to/meet with/see head teacher/rector/director/principal/headmaster/headmistress **next morning/day**.

Got spoken to by headteacher **the next day**.

   • (If no uniform,) sent home **to change**.

11. • Pupils/Kids (would have to) **agree** to it/having a uniform/pullover/jumper/sweater.
   Pupils would have to think it was OK.

   • They/The school would have to/must decide themselves what the uniform should be/look like/ what was part of the uniform.
   They have to agree on a style.

   Not a whole uniform, just a pullover
   Introduce uniform slowly by wearing just a pullover
   May have to introduce a school jumper before other uniform
   You could wear a school jumper but choose other clothes yourself
   Try just one item e.g. a jumper
   Start with a pullover

12. • (Different) uniform for each season/according to the season/time of year
   One for each season/time of year

SECTION B

Please see the table on pages 96–97 which provides details of the criteria required to produce a good essay answer.

HIGHER GERMAN
READING AND DIRECTED WRITING
2013

SECTION I – READING

1. (a) • 3 to/or 4 loads of washing **every/per/each/a day**
   3 to 4 machine washes **every day**
   She does the laundry 3 to 4 times **every day**
   Uses washing machine 3-4 times **a day**

   • 8 hours of ironing on (a) **Sunday(s)**

   (b) • A (swimming/paddling) pool **and** a sandpit/sandbox/
   crate of sand in a hut/in a Wendy/wooden house/
   playhouse
   a wooden shed to protect the indoor sandpit
   a wooden house where they can make sand-castles

2. (a) • Set/lay/prepare the table
   He is on kitchen duty/work

   • Collect/Fetch/Pick up/Meet Jonas and Anna/the 3 year
   old twins from the bus(-stop)/stop/where they get off the
   bus

   (b) • Jule tips/empties/overturns/topples/knocks/throws/
   chucks her plate/bowl/dish/food over/on the floor/
   ground/turns her plate upside down over the ground

   • Emily's plate of/with noodles/pasta/spaghetti falls onto
   the floor/falls down/gets/is knocked over

   (c) • He fills/loads (up)/stacks/stocks the dishwasher/puts the
   dishes/plates/everything in the dishwasher and
   gets/gives/hands/passes/offers/serves/makes/takes his
   mother a coffee

   • He takes/returns/brings Jonas back to the bus to go
   (back) to the Kita/day care centre/nursery as he has day
   care in the afternoon/he wants to go there

3. (a) • It promises/gives/allows/is for/It tells her she can have a
   few/couple of hours on the couch ("which she never
   gets/does")

   • He wants to/will/would take on/over/take care
   of/do/undertake/carry out the housework/house-
   keeping/household/the work that his mother would
   usually do **for a day**

   (b) • The 3 hour (long) (big) shop(ping trip) without (any)
   children

4. (a) (i) • To paint **and** (wall)paper the hall(way)(s)/corridor/
   Give the hall a coat of paint and wallpaper it/Get the
   hall painted and papered

   (ii) • Convert/Reconstruct/Renovate/Rebuild/Make
   alterations to/Refurbish/Re-do the attic/loft/Get a
   loft conversion for the **two oldest/eldest/
   older/elder brothers**/Make/Turn the attic into a
   den/room for the **two oldest brothers/boys**/The
   attic needs to get changed into a bedroom for the **two
   oldest boys**/ Build a room in the attic for the **two
   oldest boys**

   (b) • The four twins/youngsters can/will move out of/get out
   from the parents'/adults'/master bedroom
   The four twins can/will move in to/will get the free
   children's room/the free room (that the older brothers
   leave)

5. *Any two from:*
   • Emily and Jule are asleep/sleeping in the kitchen
   • Max and one of his girl-friends/a/his girl-friend are taking
   the dog a walk/out/are walking the dog/Max went for a walk
   with his girl friend and his dog
   • Joshua has gone to a friend's/is (out) at a friend's/is visiting a
   friend/has gone to see a friend

6. (a) (i) • Mum/Mother/Mam **has to/must** hold her/Jule's
   hand for a few/couple of/2 minutes

   (ii) • Dad/Father **has to/must** say 'Good Night' two or/to
   three/2-3 times

   (b) • **From** 9.30 pm/From when Joshua puts his light out
   until 6.30 am/the next morning

7. Im Haus landen Rucksäcke, Mützen und Schals auf dem
   Boden.

   In the house

   rucksacks
   backpacks

   caps
   hats

   and scarves/scarfs

   land (up)

   on the floor/ground.

   Bei acht Kindern ist der Geräuschpegel meistens sehr hoch.

   With eight/8 children/kids (around)
   At the home/house of 8 children
   In the house of 8 children
   Having 8 children means
   When you have 8 children
   With 8 children in the house

   the noise level

   is/'s

   usually/generally/mostly/mainly/normally
   most of the time
   more often than not

   very high.

   the volume….very loud

   Das kann natürlich auch nerven,

   That/This/It

   can

   of course
   naturally/certainly

   also/too/as well

   be/get annoying/irritating.
   annoy you.
   bother you.
   bug you.
   get on your/one's nerves.
   be wearing on the nerves
   hack you off.
   needle you.
   irritate (you).

aber die Mutter sieht es positiv: „Es ist Leben im Haus.

but

the mother/mum

sees/views this/that/it
looks at it

positively:
as a positive (thing):
as something positive:
as (being) positive:
from a/the positive side:
in a positive way:
the positive(s):
the positive in it

sees the positive (side):

There is life in the house.
It is lively/alive in the house.
It is lively at home.
It brings life to the house.
It brings the house to life.
It makes the house a lively place.

Ohne die Kinder würde mir etwas fehlen."

Without the children/kids

I would

be missing/lacking

something

something would be missing in my life/for me.

I would feel like I am missing something.

I would feel (like) something (was) missing.

something would be missing from/for/in me.

to me something would be missing.

There would be something missing from/in/to me.

SECTION II – DIRECTED WRITING

Category	Mark	Content	Accuracy	Language Resource – Variety, Range, Structures
Very Good	15	• All bullet points are covered fully, in a balanced way, including a number of complex sentences. • Some candidates may also provide additional information. • A wide range of verbs/verb forms, tenses and constructions is used. • Overall this comes over as a competent, well thought-out account of the event which reads naturally.	• The candidate handles all aspects of grammar and spelling accurately, although the language may contain some minor errors or even one more serious error. • Where the candidate attempts to use language more appropriate to post-Higher, a slightly higher number of inaccuracies need not detract from the overall very good impression.	• The candidate is comfortable with almost all the grammar used and generally uses a different verb or verb form in each sentence. • There is good use of a variety of tenses, adjectives, adverbs and prepositional phrases and, where appropriate, word order. • The candidate uses co-ordinating conjunctions and subordinate clauses throughout the writing. • The language flows well.
Good	12	• All bullet points are addressed, generally quite fully, and some complex sentences may be included. • The response to one bullet point may be thin, although other bullet points are dealt with in some detail. • The candidate uses a reasonable range of verbs/verb forms and other constructions.	• The candidate generally handles verbs and other parts of speech accurately but simply. • There may be some errors in spelling, adjective endings and, where relevant, case endings. • Use of accents may be less secure. • Where the candidate is attempting to use more complex vocabulary and structures, these may be less successful, although basic structures are used accurately. • There may be minor misuse of dictionary.	• There may be less variety in the verbs used. • The candidate is able to use a significant amount of complex sentences. • In one bullet point the language may be more basic than might otherwise be expected at this level. • Overall the writing will be competent, mainly correct, but pedestrian.
Satisfactory	9	• The candidate uses mainly simple, more basic sentences. • The language is perhaps repetitive and uses a limited range of verbs and fixed phrases not appropriate to this level. • In some examples, one or two bullet points may be less fully addressed. • In some cases, the content may be similar to that of good or very good examples, but with some serious accuracy issues.	• The verbs are generally correct, but basic. • Tenses may be inconsistent, with present tenses being used at times instead of past tenses. • There are quite a few errors in other parts of speech – personal pronouns, gender of nouns, adjective endings, cases, singular/plural confusion – and in the use of accents. • Some prepositions may be inaccurate or omitted eg I went the town. • While the language may be reasonably accurate in three or four bullet points, in the remaining two control of the language structure may deteriorate significantly. • Overall, there is more correct than incorrect.	• The candidate copes with the past tense of some verbs. • A limited range of verbs is used to address some of the bullet points. • Candidate relies on a limited range of vocabulary and structures. • Occasionally, the past participle is incorrect or the auxiliary verb is omitted. • Sentences may be basic and mainly brief. • There is minimal use of adjectives, probably mainly after "is" eg The boss was helpful. • The candidate has a weak knowledge of plurals. • There may be several spelling errors eg reversal of vowel combinations.

Category	Mark	Content	Accuracy	Language Resource – Variety, Range, Structures
Unsatisfactory	6	• In some cases the content may be basic. • In other cases there may be little difference in content between Satisfactory and Unsatisfactory. • The language is repetitive, with undue reliance on fixed phrases and a limited range of common basic verbs such as *to be, to have, to play, to watch*. • While the language used to address the more predictable bullet points may be accurate, serious errors occur when the candidate attempts to address the less predictable areas. • The Directed Writing may be presented as a single paragraph.	• Ability to form tenses is inconsistent. • In the use of the perfect tense the auxiliary verb is omitted on a number of occasions. • There may be confusion between the singular and plural form of verbs. • There are errors in many other parts of speech – gender of nouns, cases, singular/plural confusion, spelling and, where appropriate, word order. • Several errors are serious, perhaps showing mother tongue interference. • There may be one sentence which is not intelligible to a sympathetic native speaker. • One area may be very weak. • Overall, there is more incorrect than correct.	• The candidate copes mainly only with the predictable language required at the earlier bullet points. • The verbs "was" and "went" may also be used correctly. • There is inconsistency in the use of various expressions, especially verbs. • Sentences are more basic. • An English word may appear in the writing or a word may be omitted. • There may be an example of serious dictionary misuse.
Poor	3	• The content and language may be very basic. • However, in many cases the content may be little different from that expected at Unsatisfactory or even at Satisfactory.	• Many of the verbs are incorrect or even omitted. • There are many errors in other parts of speech – personal pronouns, gender of nouns, adjective endings, cases, singular/plural confusion, word order, spelling. • Prepositions are not used correctly. • The language is probably inaccurate throughout the writing. • Some sentences may not be understood by a sympathetic native speaker.	• The candidate cannot cope with more than 1 or 2 basic verbs, frequently *had* and *was*. • The candidate displays almost no knowledge of past tenses of verbs. • Verbs used more than once may be written differently on each occasion. • The candidate has a very limited vocabulary. • Several English or "made-up" words may appear in the writing. • There are examples of serious dictionary misuse.
Very Poor	0	• The content is very basic OR • The candidate has not completed at least three of the core bullet points.	• (Virtually) nothing is correct. • Most of the errors are serious. • Very little is intelligible to a sympathetic native speaker.	• The candidate copes only with "have" and "am". • Very few words are correctly written in the foreign language. • English words are used. • There may be several examples of mother tongue interference. • There may be several examples of serious dictionary misuse.

HIGHER GERMAN LISTENING/WRITING 2013

SECTION A

1. *Any two from:*
   - Finished (with)/Left (middle) school
     Fed up/Could not be bothered with school/Did not want to do any more school/Did not enjoy school any more/Did not want to go to school any more/Did not want to go back to school/No longer wanted to be in school/Had no desire to continue with school/education/School was not fun any more/Did not feel like staying on at school
   - (Wanted) to go/travel abroad/to another country/to a foreign country
     To work as/be/become an au-pair/nanny/child-minder
     To work abroad/in another country/Go abroad to find a job/To work and live there
   - (Had) always wanted to (come/go to Scotland)

2. (a) • They have/There are two children/kids
      - They live in a **big/large/huge** castle/chateau/palace (at the sea)
        They live in a castle in West Scotland/the west of Scotland/Argyll
        They live in Argyll in West Scotland/the west of Scotland (Must have live plus two details from big+castle+Argyll + west Scotland)
   (b) • She was supposed/meant/expected to/had to do **all** (of) the housework/the **whole** (of the) housework
        She had to clean the **whole** castle/house
        She had to do **all** the chores
        She had to do **everything** in the house
        She had to look after/tend to the **whole** house

3. (a) • They **sometimes** rent out/let out the castle (as a hotel)
        The castle/It was (also) **sometimes** a hotel
        They **sometimes** used the house as a hotel
        Twice/2 or 3 times a month the house is used as a hotel
   (b) • Move out/away with the children twice a month
        Take the children away twice a month/every two weeks/ 2 or 3 times a month/when guests were there

4. (a) • Two months (or so)
        About two months
        From September to November
   (b) • She did not like/enjoy the situation/arrangement(s)/She was not happy/pleased/comfortable with the situation/ The situation did not appeal to her/The situation was not for her/I do not like the situation
        She did not want/like to work like this/that/The work was not for her/She could not do this any more/It was not the work she wanted

5. • (They lived on/had owned) a farm/in a farm house

6. *Any one from:*
   (a) • They spent practically all the time/a lot of time/every spare minute outside/outdoors/in the fresh air/They did a lot of things outside
      - She particularly liked looking after the children, not the house/She spent more time with the children than doing the chores/She was there for the children, not the housework/She could spend her time working with the kids rather than doing the chores

   (b) *Any two from:*
      - Looked after/Cared for/Took care of/Fed the animals
      - Did things that had nothing to do with watching TV Did more practical activities instead of watching TV Did not sit around/spend time watching TV
      - **In bad weather/When the weather was not good** they made/built models/things/did something else/things in the house/inside

7. • Took/Led groups/tourists/groups of tourists up/through Rocky Mountains
     Showed tourists/groups around the Rocky Mountains/Tour guide in Rocky Mountains
     Took tourists on horseback through Rocky Mountains
     Horse-riding in the Rocky Mountains/She rode a horse in the Rocky Mountains
     She led small groups of tourists on horses
     (Answer must have two elements of tourists+horse+Rocky Mountains)

8. *Any two from:*
   - Found/Got/Rented a flat/apartment/house/somewhere to stay/accommodation/her own place to stay
   - Began/Started (her first year at) college/Went to college/ Signed up for college/Did first year of college
   - Did/Took/Sat/Got (Highers in) English, Physics and Chemistry

9. *Any one from:*
   - Studying Environmental Science/Studies/Working in Environmental Science/She is an Environmental Scientist/Studying about the environment
   - She is a second-year student/She is in the second year of her degree/studies/course/She is in (the) second year at university/college

10. *Any one from:*
    - This is what **really** interests her/It **really** interests her/She finds it **very/truly** interesting/It interests her **the most**/She has a **genuine** interest in it/She has **finally** found what interests her/This is **exactly** what interests her/It is **really** interesting/It fascinates her
    - This is the area/field she would like to work in/She definitely wants to do this as a career/She definitely wants a job in this area/This is exactly the sort of work she wants to do/This is what she wants to do/It is related to what she wants to do

11. • She got a job offer (there)
     - People have told her to get in touch/contact them/come back to Canada if/when she wants/is looking for work experience/a job
       She already has contacts in Canada
       She should let people/them know if she wanted some practical work/job

SECTION B

Category	Mark	Content	Accuracy	Language Resource – Variety, Range, Structures
Very Good	10	• The topic is covered fully, in a balanced way, including a number of complex sentences. • Some candidates may also provide additional information. • A wide range of verbs/verb forms and constructions is used. There may also be a variety of tenses. • Overall this comes over as a competent, well thought-out response to the task which reads naturally.	• The candidate handles all aspects of grammar and spelling accurately, although the language may contain some minor errors or even one more serious error. • Where the candidate attempts to use language more appropriate to post-Higher, a slightly higher number of inaccuracies need not detract from the overall very good impression.	• The candidate is comfortable with almost all the grammar used and generally uses a different verb or verb form in each sentence. • There is good use of a variety of tenses, adjectives, adverbs and prepositional phrases and, where appropriate, word order. • The candidate uses co-ordinating conjunctions and subordinate clauses throughout the writing. • The language flows well.
Good	8	• The topic is addressed, generally quite fully, and some complex sentences may be included. • The candidate uses a reasonable range of verbs/verb forms and other constructions.	• The candidate generally handles verbs and other parts of speech accurately but simply. • There may be some errors in spelling, adjective endings and, where relevant, case endings. • Use of accents may be less secure. • Where the candidate is attempting to use more complex vocabulary and structures, these may be less successful, although basic structures are used accurately. • There may be minor misuse of dictionary.	• There may be less variety in the verbs used. • Most of the complex sentences use co-ordinating conjunctions, and there may also be examples of subordinating conjunctions where appropriate. • At times the language may be more basic than might otherwise be expected at this level. • Overall the writing will be competent, mainly correct, but pedestrian.
Satisfactory	6	• The candidate uses mainly simple, more basic sentences. • The language is perhaps repetitive and uses a limited range of verbs and fixed phrases not appropriate to this level. • The topic may not be fully addressed. • In some cases, the content may be similar to that of good or very good examples, but with some serious accuracy issues.	• The verbs are generally correct, but basic. • Tenses may be inconsistent. • There are quite a few errors in other parts of speech – personal pronouns, gender of nouns, adjective endings, cases, singular/plural confusion – and in the use of accents. • Some prepositions may be inaccurate or omitted eg I go the town. • While the language may be reasonably accurate at times, the language structure may deteriorate significantly in places. • Overall, there is more correct than incorrect and there is the impression overall that the candidate can handle tenses.	• The candidate copes with the present tense of most verbs. • A limited range of verbs is used. • Candidate relies on a limited range of vocabulary and structures. • Where the candidate attempts constructions with modal verbs, these are not always successful. • Sentences may be basic and mainly brief. • There is minimal use of adjectives, probably mainly after "is" eg My friend is reliable. • The candidate has a weak knowledge of plurals. • There may be several spelling errors eg reversal of vowel combinations.

Category	Mark	Content	Accuracy	Language Resource – Variety, Range, Structures
Unsatisfactory	4	• In some cases the content may be basic. • In other cases there may be little difference in content between Satisfactory and Unsatisfactory. • The language is repetitive, with undue reliance on fixed phrases and a limited range of common basic verbs such as *to be, to have, to play, to watch*. • While the language used to address the more predictable aspects of the task may be accurate, serious errors occur when the candidate attempts to address a less predictable aspect. • The Personal Response may be presented as a single paragraph.	• Ability to form tenses is inconsistent. • In the use of the perfect tense the auxiliary verb is omitted on a number of occasions. • There may be confusion between the singular and plural form of verbs. • There are errors in many other parts of speech – gender of nouns, cases, singular/plural confusion – and in spelling and, where appropriate, word order. • Several errors are serious, perhaps showing mother tongue interference. • There may be one sentence which is not intelligible to a sympathetic native speaker. • Overall, there is more incorrect than correct.	• The candidate copes mainly only with predictable language. • There is inconsistency in the use of various expressions, especially verbs. • Sentences are more basic. • An English word may appear in the writing or a word may be omitted. • There may be an example of serious dictionary misuse.
Poor	2	• The content and language may be very basic. • However, in many cases the content may be little different from that expected at Unsatisfactory or even at Satisfactory.	• Many of the verbs are incorrect or even omitted. • There are many errors in other parts of speech – personal pronouns, gender of nouns, adjective endings, cases, singular/plural confusion – and in spelling and word order. • Prepositions are not used correctly. • The language is probably inaccurate throughout the writing. • Some sentences may not be understood by a sympathetic native speaker.	• The candidate cannot cope with more than 1 or 2 basic verbs, frequently "has" and "is". • Verbs used more than once may be written differently on each occasion. • The candidate has a very limited vocabulary. • Several English or "made-up" words may appear in the writing. • There are examples of serious dictionary misuse.
Very Poor	0	• The content is very basic	• (Virtually) nothing is correct. • Most of the errors are serious. • Very little is intelligible to a sympathetic native speaker.	• The candidate copes only with "have" and "am". • Very few words are correctly written in the foreign language. • English words are used. • There may be several examples of mother tongue interference. • There may be several examples of serious dictionary misuse